Tossing Heat

The Ken Ryan Story

by
Kenneth F. Ryan Sr.

PublishAmerica
Baltimore

© 2007 by Kenneth F. Ryan Sr.
All rights reserved. No part of this book may be reproduced, stored in a retrieval system or transmitted in any form or by any means without the prior written permission of the publishers, except by a reviewer who may quote brief passages in a review to be printed in a newspaper, magazine or journal.

First printing

ISBN: 1-4241-8015-5
PUBLISHED BY PUBLISHAMERICA, LLLP
www.publishamerica.com
Baltimore

Printed in the United States of America

Hope you
Enjoy

Kin Ryan

I dedicate this book to every kid
who ever picked up a bat and ball.

Acknowledgments

To Dr. Gilbert Woodside, a teacher at Seekonk High School and avid baseball fan, for the many hours he spent with me organizing and getting this book off the ground, for his rewriting, editing, and constantly believing that this book would be written. His lasting words after every meeting were, "Ken, keep writing, keep writing."

To another valuable friend, Russell E. Spooner, author, for his insight, ideas, and perception of the material in this story. His final corrections on every page are greatly appreciated. We affectionately named him "Russell of the Red Pen."

A special thanks to the Seekonk School System, Seekonk, Massachusetts, and Seekonk High School. Over a two-year period, we held our Writers Workshops in the high school library.

And finally, to my wife, Gloria. Her professional computer wizardry certainly made it easier for me to make words flow on my computer. Many thanks.

It rained in the morning and the sky was still overcast. There was a threat of more rain; you could feel it in the air. We were only a few minutes away from the park and I could see Kenny was anxious about getting there. The Darlington American Little League's complex was in a local public park, Slater Park. It was a short five-minute ride from our home in Pawtucket, Rhode Island. As we entered the park, we saw groups of kids on the playing fields with their fathers and coaches.

George Patrick Duffy, a Rhode Island sports legend and coach, was there organizing the day's activities. George and I had been friends for years. I introduced Kenny to him and he told us that the younger boys were using the rear ball field for their first round of tryouts.

As we walked around the several fields in the park, I noticed many fathers who I knew during my own childhood. I started talking to one of the fathers that lived in my neighborhood when I was a young boy. I recall this individual as being a good ballplayer during his high school days. He had his son Jerry with him. The father told me that Jerry was in his second year of Little League. He was playing with the ten-, eleven-, and twelve-year-old kids. He was two years older than Kenny. Jerry was a tall boy and muscular. He wore his team uniform and one could see it was recently washed and pressed nicely. He looked proud in it. Slung over his right shoulder was his equipment bag. Popping out of the front of the bag was a baseball bat. His dad told me that Jerry was excited about the upcoming year and expected to have another good year. He said Jerry made the all-star team last year and was lights out on the mound. Jerry looked up at his dad and had a smile on his face. It was easy to see that both were proud of what had been accomplished by the youngster. I informed my neighbor this was Ken's first year playing Little League, but I was sure he would be able to handle himself satisfactorily. I told him I was working with Kenny on his throwing to the bases, and on pitching. I intended to have Ken go out for pitching since he had a strong arm. I noticed Jerry was standing by his father's side and was staring at Ken. Ken was eyeballing this kid too. I wondered what they were thinking; both kids had no real expression on their faces. However, during the time the neighbor and I were discussing baseball the boys never talked. Just a blank stare between them. It reminded me of two gunslingers, Jack Wilson and Shane out on the plains knowing they would meet someday in a showdown. However, there never was a showdown between the two boys, and they never met again. It appeared to me both boys were feeling each other out, Jerry with the temperament of intimidating the younger kid. Ken held his own and did not get rattled or embarrassed. Later we moved out of state, and into a new Little League program. I often wondered what would have happened if these two boys ever faced off against each other. Jerry later made every all-star team during his Little League days. I never heard of him after that, but was told by a baseball coach Jerry quit playing baseball.

  This was Kenny's first tryout for a Little League team. I knew he was uneasy about it; kids are always a bit apprehensive at spring tryouts anyway and the first one is always the most nerve-wracking. The kids worry about misjudging a fly ball, letting a grounder go through their legs or failing to hit. If this happens to you, you feel that all of the other kids are better than you. That they field, throw and hit better and are more aggressive than you. I tried to explain to him just be yourself, concentrate and do your best when it comes your turn. I went over the things we had worked on almost daily for three years. I reminded him, "Catch the ball in the center of your glove, stay in the batter's box and don't be afraid of the ball." We had hundreds of hours practicing fielding, hitting and pitching. I knew he had a strong arm for an eight-year-old. The dream of becoming a Major Leaguer starts here with the anxious kids and their hopeful dads. Certainly, some dads believe that their sons can make it to "the show" (big leagues). Most parents think their kids are all-stars, regardless of their actual talent. Every dad wants his kid to be either the starting pitcher or the shortstop…both "glory" spots on a team.

Kenny was born October 24, 1968. He was our third child and only son. Cheryl and Brenda, our daughters, were good athletes and played for the Pawtucket Slaterettes, an all-girl baseball team. The girls pitched well for their team. When it came to baseball, now that I think about it, Kenny was a natural. That word is and was used frequently though not always applied appropriately. Naturals always seemed to hit the ball farther, threw harder and were always involved in the big play of the game. The way they stood at the plate, the command of their pitches, or their flair at turning an inning double play told you the "natural" had something others didn't have. Their confidence and ability were clearly evident.

At eight years old, Ken made the nine- and ten-year-old all-star team. The second year he played shortstop and pitched for the Fountains, a local band that sponsored his first Little League team. He pitched well that year. He overpowered opposing batters with an incredible fastball. The following year (1978) we moved to the neighboring town of Seekonk, Massachusetts. Sadly, this move kept him from playing in the Darlington Little League. He now entered the Seekonk Little League system.

Tryouts for the Seekonk Little League were held in March. It was cold and very windy that day. Ken had to prove himself once again. Unlike the situation in Pawtucket, we hadn't lived long enough in Seekonk for me to meet and get to know any of the fathers or coaches. Tryouts started at 8:00 a.m., and the fields were packed with kids, parents, coaches and league officials. Each kid would get a chance at fielding grounders, pop-ups and then take a few swings at the plate.

Ken was a big ten-year-old trying out for a team of eleven- and twelve-year-olds in the Major League Division. If he didn't make a Major Division team he'd be dropped to the Farm Division. This division consisted of teams of much younger kids. I knew Ken would be very disappointed if he didn't make a Major Division team. His one advantage was his size. He would fit in with the older guys with no problem. Ken didn't impress any of the coaches. He let a couple of grounders get by him and he looked as though he had never swung at a ball before, missing several pitches right over the plate.

I was told by some of the fathers that because of the large numbers of boys trying out for the Major Division teams some wouldn't make it and be dropped to the Farm Division. Even this division was getting full as organized baseball became very popular in Seekonk.

During the ride home, Ken asked me how I thought he did. I told him, "You picked a bad day to miss pitches over the plate and not field well." The one thing that might save him from the minors was his cannon of an arm. He had thrown some balls from the centerfield fence all the way to the catcher at home plate. I heard some of the coaches ask, "Who is the kid with the rifle for an arm?" Neither of us thought he would make a Major Division team.

Several days later, I received a call from one of the league officials informing me that Kenny had been selected by a Major Division team, Seekonk Oil. After the first few games the new kid playing for Seekonk Oil was being recognized as a good hitter and a pitcher who was almost un-hittable. Those that did manage to get hits off him that year were some of the best twelve-year-olds. Poor fielding by his team cost him a perfect season. At the plate he hit five (5) home runs and was consistently on base. It was a very good first year in Seekonk.

He exploded on the scene his second year on the team. He continued to be un-hittable and won all of his starts. He dominated the league on and off the mound. In addition to his incredible pitching, he belted a league-leading 25 home runs. We believe his homerun record still stands. His third year was more of the same. He continued to put fear in the hearts of opposing batters; they hated to get into the batter's box to face him. Ken threw the ball so hard that during an all-star game, parents petitioned the umpire in an attempt to keep Kenny from pitching. They feared that one of his fastballs would get away from him and do serious injury to someone. The petition was denied and Ken pitched the entire game for the win.

His last year of Little League ball was impressive. He won all of his starts, had a high on-base percentage and hit eleven home runs in spite of the fact that most teams wouldn't pitch to him. Ken was an all-star all through Little League. One of the coaches from the Little League, Al Hunt, also managed and sponsored the Seekonk All Stars. Al was a real baseball guy and loved the game as much as I did. The Seekonk All Stars went on the road as a traveling team playing other all-star teams from all over New England. We played baseball right up until the start of school in September.

Hunt and some of the other fathers could not wait until the regular season ended. We then began to select the all-star team. These players were the best on their team and only two were going to be selected. This took place after the all-star game and sometimes took two weeks. Hunt would then take his all-stars that now were the Seekonk traveling team and traveled all over New England. We made stops in the Boston area and Cape Cod. We visited cities and towns in Maine, Vermont, and New Hampshire. I sometimes think it was the best years for Kenny. It certainly was great training for him and he was able to pitch often and harness his pitching arm. He threw many innings with the traveling team, and I believed it helped him when he went to the regulation field when he turned thirteen. When kids can play baseball for the entire summer it only makes than better when they grow older. Some of these boys went onto college and excelled on their baseball teams. The three years we played with the traveling team, we won more games than we lost. We had cookouts in some of the parks close by, or on the grounds of the motels we stayed in. The kids all headed for the swimming pool right after the games. The weather was hot since the games were played in mid-summer. That last year we played for Hunt's team, he bought all the kids baseball jackets. There was not a sponsor for the team, and I knew he took the money out of his own pocket to pay for them. He was a generous person as well as being one of the real good people in Little League baseball. His dream was to make it to Williamsport, and play in the Little League World Series. We just did not have the players to reach that plateau.

When Ken turned thirteen, he started playing Babe Ruth Baseball. Babe Ruth ball is played on a major-league-size field. Bases are 90 feet apart and the pitchers mound is 60 feet 6 inches from home plate. The rules are the same as major league ball too. Many kids get discouraged at this level simply because of the bigger playing field. Kids who hit home runs in Little League were hitting only doubles and long fly-outs on the major-league-sized fields. Some found the bigger fields slowed the game and made it a bit more boring. Ken was anxious to test his skills. He was ready mentally and physically for this new and bigger challenge. He had little trouble adjusting to a bigger and more competitive baseball environment.

I always believed that Ken would benefit from playing against older players. I was able to get him into the Rhode Island Amateur League at age fifteen. The league is made up of former ball players from high school and college. There were a number of good players in the league. Ken played two years for a club out of Cranston. He was pitching against hitters three to twenty years his senior. I tried to have him pitch part of a game three times a week. If he started a game he then would come in to relieve in one or two others. I felt this would help strengthen him arm.

Between amateur and legion ball he was kept pretty busy and never lacked for enough pitching in a given week. At sixteen Kenny was the youngest player attending a baseball camp sponsored by the Atlanta Braves in Connecticut. That day when we returned to Seekonk we decided to go to the Seekonk Middle School field and watch a Pony League game.

One of the legion coaches was there and we told him about the Connecticut camp. The coach said, off-handedly, that kids from Seekonk just don't make it in professional sports. Unfortunately, Ken was standing beside me when the comment was made. I'm sure that he was just stating the facts but I could sense that Ken was uneasy about the statement. As we drove home I told him to continue to play great baseball and good things can happen.

We had to decide on a high school for Ken. Some of his teammates went to LaSalle Academy in Providence, Rhode Island, or St Raphael Academy in Pawtucket, Rhode Island, both had good athletic programs and excelled in baseball. I wanted Ken to go to Seekonk High School; it too had a good athletic program. I felt Ken could flourish in a small suburban school and would easily stand out in a good small school sports program. I wasn't wrong!

As Ken was growing up, he was always doing something to keep himself busy. If it wasn't sports it would be reading a good book. He learned how to play tennis and became good at it. After a short time playing, he was able to beat many older guys. He loved most sports. He attempted ice-skating when he was eight but soon learned that he was not going to be a figure skater so he gave it up. Thus, ice hockey did not become one of Ken's favorite sports.

His first year at Seekonk High School was a comfortable transition for Ken. He was with many of his Little League and Babe Ruth teammates and friends from the neighborhood. His pitching continued to improve and he played well his freshman year. It was in his sophomore year that his pitching really became noticeable. He won his first five games and looked unbeatable, even though the team faltered during the middle of the season. Unfortunately, the Seekonk team was weak. Only five seniors backed Ken's efforts, the rest of the team were sophomores like him.

Tom Ridolfi, head baseball coach and teacher at Seekonk, told the press that he had never seen a pitcher with an arm as strong as Ken's. He was impressed with Ken's ability to get batters out.

Ken played one season of American Legion baseball. This league is made up of the best high school players. Not all kids make the team because the level of play is so high. Some kids make a team but sit on the bench waiting for a chance to play. Kenny made the Bristol, Rhode Island, team as a starting pitcher. The coaches were a father-and-son team, the Annarummos. The son, Steve, had played minor league ball for the Red Sox. They were good coaches and made baseball exciting that season. Ken went 7-2 that year but the team lost in the playoffs. He gained a lot of valuable experience that really helped him in his final year at Seekonk High School.

In his senior year, his fastball was clocked at 87 and 90 mph. His curve ball was a good setup for his fastball. That good curve made his fastball look even faster than it really was. In three years at Seekonk his ERA was around 2.00 and was touted as the best pitcher to ever come out of the school. His hitting, however, dropped as he became a regular starting pitcher. He concentrated on his pitching and shutting opposing batters down. He let his teammates worry about hitting and scoring runs. I told him that "hitting .380+ in high school is not that unusual. Most of those heavy hitters never make it to the 'bigs' (major leagues). Decent hitters are a dime a dozen. It's good pitchers who ink the big contracts."

By his senior year Ken was a big kid at six feet four inches and 205 pounds. Ken's senior year was his best. The team expected a lot out of him and he delivered. Prior to the start of the season, the head coach was interviewed by the local papers about the upcoming season. He told the reporters that it would be up to Kenny to carry the team. This now put an enormous amount of pressure on him. He knew that he had to put up very good numbers. The article didn't help team spirit but the team rallied behind him in every start he made.

Ken and I were at Fenway Park watching Oil Can Boyd pitch. The park was packed as usual and Ken was impressed with Boyd's pitching. As we were leaving the park Ken turned to me and said, "Dad, someday I'm going to pitch at Fenway." Little did we know that in a few weeks major league and college scouts would be giving him high marks on the "try to sign" lists.

In April the team had a game against Bourne on Cape Cod. Ken was at his best. He pitched a no-hitter and struck out sixteen batters. He struck out the side in the first, second and fourth innings and didn't allow a ball out of the infield. He followed this gem up with a game that brought him real notice.

In this game Kenny struck out 21 batters in an eleven-inning game on the same day Roger Clemens broke the major league record by striking out 20 batters in a nine-inning game.

The local press had a field day touting the fact that Ken had one more strikeout than Clemens. From this point on major league and college scouts, in droves, were at every game Kenny pitched. They wanted to get a close look at the big kid with "heat." Letters were coming in from many college baseball coaches from around the country. One in particular, the University of Maine Black Bears, offered him a scholarship and we were set on accepting it.

Ken still had the season to finish for Seekonk. At all of his remaining starts, I noticed a man sitting near the backstop directly behind home plate. I knew he was involved somehow in baseball but wasn't sure if he was a coach or scout. We never spoke, but he was always there. When I asked Coach Ridolfi, he told me that the man was Bill Enos, a longtime scout for the Boston Red Sox. Enos had signed some very good Massachusetts players including Rich Gedman from

Worcester. Scouts were constantly inquiring about Ken's future. "Is Ken going to college or turn pro?" they'd ask. It was our intention that Ken would go to college and get a good education. I let the pro scouts know that Ken wouldn't be signing baseball contracts at this time. Scouts attending Ken's final starts grew fewer and fewer until only one remained.

The pro baseball draft was held in June. Ken was not drafted because scouts felt he'd be too difficult to sign, so why waste a pick? In spite of our stance on Ken's college future, we still were disappointed that he was not selected. At Ken's next start, Bill Enos was sitting in his usual place behind the backstop at home plate. He talked to us at the end of every game about signing a minor league contract with the Red Sox. Our thoughts were beginning to change; college possibly could be put on hold. Ken could play ball and go to college during the off-season. The Black Bears of the University of Maine would have to wait. In June of 1986, at the age of seventeen, Ken Ryan signed a contract with the Boston Red Sox, the team he loved, the team he grew up with, and the team he predicted he would pitch for.

A few days after signing he turned in his American Legion uniform. There were some surprised players and coaches. Most thought he was on his way to Maine. Coach Annarummo had the team sign a ball for Ken as they gathered around him to wish him good luck. Some said they'd see him next on the mound at Fenway.

My wife had her doubts about Ken's relationship with pro baseball. She believed that he should attend college in September, play college baseball and work on earning his degree. She felt the odds were against Ken making it in the big leagues and she felt an education would be a great backup. She never developed an interest in baseball so…. There were many discussions about Ken and baseball at our dinner table. It's strange because, even today, she still thinks Ken should have gone to college and earned a degree. Perhaps she was right in her way of thinking, but since recognizing Ken's ability, I intended that he get into professional baseball early on. Some ballplayers who reach the major leagues get their degrees during their playing careers.

Ken was big for his age. Size is an advantage in most sports. Kenny was always in the best of shape. As a Little Leaguer his size and ability always placed him in a position of authority. Other players looked to him because he knew what had to be done to be a winning team. When he wasn't pitching, he was at shortstop, a position he enjoyed.

His strong arm, speed, good glove (good fielder) and quick reactions made him a natural shortstop. In high school, he was also a splendid outfielder, getting to many balls that looked like they should be base hits. But, we soon began to understand that his future would be on the pitcher's mound. Kenny's final year at Seekonk High School was astounding. He pitched 97 innings and struck out 141 batters. This was quite a feat for a seventeen-year-old kid playing high school baseball. I don't believe there was a high school pitcher in the country that could match Kenny's accomplishments that year. Every time the coach asked him to take the mound, he went willingly. His arm was strong the entire year and never worried about arm problems. He knew too, that the team depended on him and it was his obligation to get the job done. The Seekonk High team was not a strong team that year. But that didn't matter to Kenny; he just wanted to pitch his team into the playoffs...which he did. The team lost in the second round. Kenny didn't pitch that game because he pitched the day before.

Reflecting on his high school career, Kenny told me it's at the high school level when baseball gets really competitive. It's here that the truly good ball players continue to shine. Many former Little League all-stars fail to play well at the high school level. They now find themselves riding the bench. Not being a star or starting player is hard to swallow. Some players lose interest and decide to leave the game.

Baseball was always fun for Ken. Baseball will continue to be as much a part of his life as it had been since his first tryout as an eight-year-old.

After high school graduation, we took the six-hour drive from Seekonk to Elmira. Elmira is a small town in upstate New York and the home of the Red Sox rookie team, the Pioneers. The Pioneers play a short season of 78 games in the New York Penn League. The league consists of several teams from the upstate New York area. We got to the ballpark about 4:00 p.m. As Ken walked on to the field, he was greeted by manager Bill Limoncelli. Limoncelli told him to get dressed immediately as he pointed to a clubhouse which didn't appear to be much larger than an average living room. Limoncelli and Ken walked toward the clubhouse. I followed behind. The manager opened the door so Kenny could enter. I had made up my mind I wanted to be alongside my son at this happy time. As I was about to step inside of the clubhouse, Limoncelli stopped me at the door and told me I was not allowed inside. Only players and coaches were allowed into the clubhouse. I was really surprised by the actions of the manager and wanted to inform him my son might need me. I thought the matter over and it finally came to me that my son was a professional now and he needed to be on his own. I would only make him feel uncomfortable being in there.

When Ken emerged from the clubhouse in his Red Sox uniform, Limoncelli informed him that he wouldn't be pitching for a while. The reason… Ken was only seventeen and would be away from home for a couple of months. The team wanted him to adjust to his new way of life.

KENNETH F. RYAN SR.

Ken walked onto the playing field and joined another new young pitcher, Curt Schilling. Schilling had reported a week earlier than Ken. The two began working out with a session of "soft toss" designed to loosen up their arms. Little did they know that their paths would cross the following year in North Carolina when both pitched for the Greensboro Hornets and later in their careers with the Philadelphia Phillies. I vividly remember that day. As we were leaving for home Ken said to me, "Dad, I'm going to make you proud of me." I responded, "You already have."

He didn't get a chance to pitch in a game for about two weeks. It was usually a losing cause. That year he pitched 21 and 2/3 innings and his record was 5-5. Not a bad start but not a stellar one either. The Pioneers had 35 players, mostly draftees and a few free agents. Major league teams carry 25 players. It is only the outstanding minor leaguer who will make it to the truly professional level. Only three of those 35 would eventually make it to the majors; third baseman Scott Cooper and pitchers Curt Schilling and Ken Ryan. All three would, at one time in their careers, play for the parent club, the Boston Red Sox.

Ken's second year in the majors at Greensboro was a real struggle. He soon realized that he wasn't pitching against high school kids anymore. Opposing batters hit him hard and he was removed from the starting rotation and moved to the bullpen. Manager Dick Berardino told Ken he had to "pitch" his way back into the rotation. Though he was really struggling he told me that he wasn't depressed over his pitching and he still had his good fastball. That was one thing about him all through his minor league years: he never gave up on himself and never thought about quitting. Ken knew that the secret of pitching was taking *command*; that is, being able to consistently throw the ball where you wanted it to go. There were many "junk ball pitchers" who have been successful at the major league level. They could throw their "junk" where it needed to go to get batters out. It's not how hard you throw; it's the movement and placement of the ball on each pitch. Command is something you learn, and it takes a long time to have major league command. Ken said, "Some pitchers throw 95-plus miles per hour and still get hit hard. They haven't learned to place the ball in the right spots and haven't got much movement on their pitches. The pitches come across the plate flat and straight. No matter how hard you throw, batters will eventually be able to 'catch up' with your pitch… Ya gotta have movement and placement to be effective. That being said, it doesn't hurt a pitcher to have a 95 mph fastball to mix in with a good curve or other sharp-breaking pitch. When you have command of the mound you are known as a pitcher…you want to be a pitcher, not a thrower. The minor leagues are full of throwers. They remain mostly unheralded and are forced to give up the dream of all minor leaguers ….making it to the major leagues."

Ken spent seven years in the minor leagues. The first five years in the minors was a difficult time for him. It was a learning process. He had to learn to live the life of ballplayers, to eat a steady diet of fast foods and endure six months away from home. Ken had a great work ethic; he always arrived at the park early for practice and extra workouts. He enjoyed his teammates and had an excellent rapport with them. Kenny was one of those guys who wasn't a wise guy and always spoke the truth. In those early years, he knew his managers and teammates had doubts about his ability. When he was announced as the starting pitcher he knew there were teammates who wished he was still in the bullpen. He was hurt by this but he also knew that he was the only one who could change things. He always lost more games than he won and carried a high earned run average (ERA) of more than five. He was terrible and he knew it. He said the way to determine a pitcher's effectiveness is to compare the innings pitched to the hits given up in those innings. If the number of hits is higher than the number of innings pitched, in most cases the pitcher would have a high ERA. Ken fell prey to this pitcher's curse. He knew his teammates began to wonder, out loud, if he should be on the team. It came to a point that for the first time in his career, he doubted himself. Also he felt it was difficult to take the mound not knowing what was going to occur. If you can't get batters out here in the low minors, how are you going to get them out in the show?

He wondered what the Red Sox management thought. Was he destined to languish in the minors as thousands of others had before him, never reaching their dream, in spite of years of practice and dedication?

Every time he pitched, he hoped his fortunes would change. He wanted this day to be the one that everything clicked and he would shut down the opposing batters. He would show his manager, the team and most important he would show the organization that he could pitch. He kept thinking to himself, *Perhaps this is the night I will turn everything around.* He still maintained that desire to go out there on the mound and compete. It never entered his mind to call it quits, pack his bags and come home. "I'm here until they boot me out."

Each spring training was the same, he was still a starter. Now, however, he was no longer the youngest player in camp and everyone knew him. After years in the minors he still hadn't proved himself. The Red Sox front office hadn't said anything about his pitching. After the miserable 6-14 1990 season, a season in which he set a new franchise record for losses, Ken had real doubts. During the off-season we (the family) knew that Ken was questioning his abilities and truly pondered his future in baseball. He talked about the grueling twelve-hour bus rides to away games that seem to suck out the strength and will to play. Perpetual minor leaguers have no future; they make little money and are given very few benefits, all for the slim hope of making a major league team. Most minor league ballplayers have part-time jobs during the season and full-time jobs in the off-season. Raising a family on minor league pay is next to impossible. All of this led to Ken's apprehension.

Trying to ease his tensions, we joked around the house about his franchise record for losses. He said that that dubious record might stand for many years. Ken was at a pivotal point in his career.

Kenny's dream was to reach the Boston AAA club in Pawtucket, Rhode Island, the PawSox. If he could make this team the next step would be the major league team the Boston Red Sox. The PawSox played at McCoy Stadium. Ken had played there during his high school and American Legion days. He dreamt about pitching in front of the hometown crowd, his friends and family from Pawtucket and Seekonk. Playing for the PawSox would give his career a real boost. This dream seemed very tenuous at this point in time.

In 1989 Ken was with the Winter Haven team and one night after a game he and a few of the players went out to a local nightclub. It was during that evening out that he met a young lady, Odalys Rodriguez. They dated for a couple of years and were married in Lakeland, Florida, 1991. They have three daughters, Julia, Amanda and Kelli Rose.

His record in 1989 with the Florida State League was 8-8. He pitched 137 innings and allowed 114 hits. Most impressive was that his ERA dropped two runs per game to 3.15. This is a very respectable ERA even at the major league level. He had a turnaround game the following year against the Durham (North Carolina) Bulls. He pitched a one-hit shutout in a 3-0 victory. He had ten strikeouts while walking only two. This was his first shutout since high school; his confidence got a real boost that night. However, that one good game was not enough and Ken knew it. It had none of the Red Sox brass convinced that he could improve. Ken was just surviving while two others who came up with him were doing well. Schilling was traded to the Baltimore franchise and Scott Cooper was in AA ball at New Britain and knocking the cover off of the ball.

Spring training was more of the same for Ken. He was hit hard and often and he walked more than he struck out. He got fewer and fewer pitching opportunities; in effect he was put on the back burner by his managers. He really began to feel that a release was in the near future. Release could come at anytime during spring training. Most players take it hard; some grovel for another chance; many feel that they have failed at the game they worked so long and so hard for. For most there is sadness, for others anger. Released players have little chance of being picked up by another club. If you were any good your original club would have kept you; your record as a ballplayer is known to all. Professional baseball for those released is a huge uncertainty. Few ballplayers have been taken off of the "scrap heap" and made it.

Those who are just plain terrible are cut quickly while others hang on until the last days while managers, the front office and player development people give the players a final look in an attempt to try to start the season with the strongest team possible. Lee Stang, the pitching coordinator, was in camp for that 1991 spring training at Fort Meyers, Florida. During one of the many meetings held during the spring camp to evaluate players and their future with the organization, Stang was to have an enormous impact on Ken's career. The Winter Haven manager knew Ken's make-up and pitching history and wanted no part of him on the team. He spoke openly that Ken was struggling and wasn't going anywhere in the organization. After a lengthy discussion about Ken's past performance it was decided that it might be in the best interest of the Red Sox to release him. He hadn't improved during his five-year minor league stint. Those in charge of player development held little hope for his improvement. They felt that if they released him now, at 21, he could still go to college and get his life in order. This at least was evidence that the organization actually cared about their players. Stang spoke up in Ken's defense, citing that he was still young and had been around for a while; it might be a good idea to keep him around for another year and change his role. In Stang's opinion, Ken should be moved from a starting role to that of a reliever. Some of those present thought that it was a waste of time and would take the place on a roster that could be used for another prospect. Ed Kenny, Sr., director of player development, thought for a moment and then agreed with Stang. Though being dropped back to single A ball at Winter Haven, Ken's career in pro baseball would see another season.

Just prior to his salvation due to the baseball savvy of Lee Stang, Ken called home to say that he expected to be released. All of the indicators were there; his poor performances, his friends and some of his past managers were reluctant to speak to him. He said, "When people sense that you are going to be released, they stay away from you. I think they fear it might happen to them too." The thought of being released is a depressing one so avoidance of one so obviously on the way out is an attempt to hopefully dodge the bullet yourself. Ken's future truly looked bleak.

Ken, happily, called home with the news that he wasn't going to be released. He said he had a meeting with Lee Stang the next morning. Stang told Kenny what transpired at the meeting and what the Red Sox wanted from him. He was definitely going to the bullpen and would only pitch in relief. No more starts for him; if the game was close he probably wouldn't get the call to the mound. The manager's lack of confidence in him was obvious…but he was still in pro ball.

His first appearance in relief that year seemed to justify the manager's opinion. He gave up a double that scored the winning run. He recalled what went through his head as he drove home to his new bride. *No way will they let me continue to pitch for this team,* he thought. *I know I'm going to get the axe any day now,* he told himself. Thinking about his career, he wondered what went wrong. This game isn't about luck; it's about being prepared and mentally strong. Oddly, the axe didn't fall; he pitched a few more games but always gave up runs. The manager pitched him only when he absolutely needed to. The team went into West Palm Beach for several games. In the first game with bases loaded Ken was called to the mound. Was this the way the manager would put the final nail in his coffin? Ken said he felt like he was pitching in the seventh game of the World Series. His first three pitches were balls, not a good start. Before the next pitch he walked off to the rear of the mound and bowed his head and prayed, "God, I need your help, I'm taking all of the pressure off of myself and giving it to you. I can't take any more and don't know what to do." His chat with God continued, "Whatever my path is I can handle it. If I am to be out of baseball that's okay, but I'm sick of this heartbreak every night I pitch." He felt a strange kind of relief, a peacefulness come over his body. His attitude changed and he told himself that whatever happened from this point on he'd be okay. "I'm not worrying anymore."

He returned to the mound and stared in at the batter. His next three pitches were strikes. He had stopped the opponents' rally dead and that coffin nail. As he reached the dugout, the manager told him he was finished for the night and to hit the showers.

When Ken arrived home, he told his wife Odalys what had occurred at the ballpark. He told her he was done worrying about the future and was not going to let the manager or anyone else get in his way. He was just going out there and pitch and see what happens. "We are going to be just fine," he told her.

He pitched several more games and his pitching was suddenly coming around. In fact, he won a few games. He suddenly seemed to be throwing harder. He was blowing opposing batters away with his newly discovered "heat." After one of the games, his catcher told him that he was throwing real fast now. The radar guns were consistently clocking him at over 90 miles per hour. One of the players showed Ken the radar gun stopped at 93 miles per hour. That was the fastest he had ever thrown in his life! His strikeouts-to-walk ratio rose dramatically. He was simply blowing hitters away. By June his ERA was a miniscule 2.05. After pitching in 21 games for the Winter Haven team, he was called up to New Britain, Connecticut. Ken had risen a notch in the professional baseball world to AA ball. Quite a change of fortunes. Al hunt from Ken's Little League days called me at 6:00 a.m. to tell me he had just heard on the radio that Ken was being promoted to New Britain.

As he entered the clubhouse to meet his new manager, he met an unhappy Larry Allen. Allen was his manager in the disastrous 6-14 season and not pleased to have Kenny added to his roster. His first outing with New Britain was against the Albany Yankees. He pitched three brilliant innings, striking out five and giving up only one hit.

The entire Ryan family made the long trip to Albany for the game in hopes that Ken would get a chance to pitch. It was a grand night to see Ken pitch so well. We spoke to him about his greatly improved pitching and he could not explain it. All of a sudden, he started throwing harder and getting hitters out. His strikeouts were really adding up and he felt so much better on the mound now. Ken told us after that game he felt he could pitch in this league and get batters out.

He told me that he finally felt comfortable on the mound and that he felt sure of himself. Ken pitched 50 innings that year for New Britain. Manager Allen had to change his tune…he was now happy to have Ken on his team. What manager wouldn't want a pitcher with a fastball above 90 mph and a microscopic 1.73 ERA? Hitters could not touch him. After one game, Ken was called into the manager's office. *This is it,* he thought, *I'm getting my release.* Allen told him to sit down, he had good news for him. Allen asked, "Do you know how to get to Pawtucket?"

Ken replied, "Yes, of course. I was born there."

The manager sat back in his chair and said, "Get your things together, you've made it to AAA Pawtucket and they want you as soon as possible."

Ken was stunned; it was so hard to believe *he was on his way to Pawtucket.* In the face of all of his disappointments and setbacks he had made three jumps in classification from A to AA to AAA ball and to the team he dreamed of pitching for and the city he longed to pitch in all in a single season.

As Ken drove through Connecticut, he tried to remember who the Pawtucket manager was; he remembered it was Butch

Hobson. Hobson had also managed the New Britain team. Hobson was a fan favorite when he played third base for the Boston Red Sox. His hard-nosed, all-out kind of play endeared him to the Red Sox faithful. He came to play every night. His managerial style reflected his playing style. His teams played hard all the time. It was a fact that it was Hobson's way or the highway. Ken liked that kind of ballplayer, team and attitude.

Ken said when ballplayers spend too many years in the minor leagues they get stagnant and some lose their competitive edge and enthusiasm for the game. Hobson was a real taskmaster and gritty manager who demanded 100% effort at all times. He did not want to hear excuses or players feeling sorry for themselves about a batting or pitching slump or lack of playing time. Stagnant players found it difficult to meet those demands and to spend night after night in the same high-energy environment was grueling. This kind of pressure and knowing that you probably have reached your highest level in professional baseball can tear a player up.

As he drove, Kenny reflected back to the night in June when he inexplicably "found" his command on the mound. He basked in that wonderful confident feeling that he could once again get batters out almost at will. He warmed to the memories of having teammates, coaches and the manager congratulate him after a strong and successful effort on the mound. This kind of thing hadn't happened much in his prior pitching performances. He was overwhelmed with the feeling of inner peace and self-confidence. He knew all he had to do from now on was to take the mound and pitch as Kenny Ryan can pitch. He could only give 100% and not worry about anything else. He was finally relaxed.

Ken wondered what was responsible for this wonderful personal transformation after more than five long years in pro ball. Why now? Who was responsible for it? He mused, *Could there be angels in the infield since there were movies about angels in the outfield?* As he drove into the parking lot of McCoy Stadium, the home of the PawSox, Ken said to himself, *This is Triple A, the PawSox. It's only 50 minutes from Fenway Park the home of the major league team.* It took Ken five and a half years to get back to the city of his birth and the ballpark where he spent many summer evenings watching the PawSox play, the ballpark where he dreamed his own baseball dreams.

As he entered the clubhouse, he saw several players he had played with in single A ball. Dave Milstein was one of them. Ken had played with Milstein at Elmira. Milstein was an infielder who had batted his way to the triple A team. The area press had noted that a local player, Ken Ryan, had finally come home.

Ken was called on to pitch on a Sunday afternoon in August. As he took the mound, he noticed that the stadium was pretty much filled to capacity. More than six thousand fans looked on. In the last inning, Ken fanned the first batter and got the next two hitters to bounce weakly to the mound for a 1-2-3 inning. Ken pitched four innings for the win. As he walked off the mound at the end of the game he was met with a loud standing ovation from the large crowd. What a great sight to see.

In the newspapers the next day Hobson was quoted as saying that Ken had only gone two innings in the past, but he was pitching so well out there, he thought he'd leave him in to finish the game.

Ken finished the season with the PawSox and couldn't wait for spring training. Ken and I spoke often about his pitching, teams and his mindset. He really liked Pawtucket. He explained that conditions were good there. How well the team owner, Ben Mondor, and team president, Mike Tamburro, treated the players. How they would both go out of their way for the team and individual players. According to Ken, "The PawSox organization was a real class act." The best part about being with the PawSox was that he was only one step from the major leagues (Boston Red Sox) and only five minutes from his home in Seekonk, Massachusetts.

The PawSox have a great slogan, *Where the Dreams Begin*. For hundreds of thousands of kids who over the years have watched games at McCoy Stadium, it is a wonderful dream. For Ken Ryan it was a dream come true. Ken said good things happen if you work hard enough and continue to have faith in yourself. He said, "I got down on myself, was depressed, and doubted but *NEVER GAVE UP*! I worked to make my dream come true."

The wait for the 1992 spring training camp was a long one. Ken couldn't wait to get back on the mound. He told me that if he pitched real well during spring training he *might* make the Boston team. He felt certain that his day on the lower rungs of the professional baseball ladder were over. No more single or double A ball for him. This great change in self-confidence was a wonderful surprise for family and friends. Ken had a very good spring training and was shocked when he was sent back to double A ball at New Britain. He was told at the end of spring training that he would make an excellent reliever because of his fastball and his newly acquired sharp-breaking curve ball. He would be the closer for the New Britain team. Happily, before he left Pawtucket the Red Sox organization told him that they were pleased with his pitching and that if he continued to pitch well he would be brought back up to Pawtucket. There was a lot of pressure on him to pitch as he never pitched before…could he handle the pressure? Ken said, "Just give me the ball." This is the baseball equivalent of saying, "You bet your ass I can!"

At least this wasn't the spring training camps of old where he had no idea of what the Red Sox organization thought of him or their plans for him. There was a bright light at the end of the tunnel between the dugout and locker room, not the dimness of uncertainty.

Ken returned to New Britain with a mission...to pitch himself back to Pawtucket and then to Boston. He was in great shape and his arm felt great. Ken hoped his pitching would bring good results. He knew too, that he would be pitching one inning, the ninth. Closer must throw strikes and minimize the walks (base on balls). You have to shut down the opposing offense by stopping late-inning rallies and keep runners off base. To be an effective closer you have to have a hard-biting fastball and a very good curve or a change-up. In 1992, Ken had that hard fastball and the sharp-breaking curve; later in his career he would develop a good change-up. For all pitchers too many lost games meant your role with the team would change. Ken realized that closers had to have a short memory; they couldn't bemoan a loss between starts like a starter can. A closer can blow (lose) a game on Tuesday and be called to pitch an inning or two on Wednesday. Closers did not have the luxury or misfortune to be able to dwell on the last losing performance.

Ken continued to pitch well for New Britain and relished his new role. That year he pitched 50.2 innings, striking out 51 and posting a major-league-like 1.95 ERA. He also set a club record of 22 saves. His call to Pawtucket came in August. Boston's great former shortstop, Rico Petrocelli, was now the Pawtucket manager. Ken was reunited with old friends Milstein, Jeff Plympton and Scott Taylor. Taylor and Ken played on the New Britain team. Taylor, a lefty, was doing a good job at Pawtucket with his knuckle-curve and a good fastball. Taylor was a control pitcher; he could throw all of his pitches for strikes. At the end of every season Taylor had a low ERA and Ken knew that someday Scott would make the bigs (major leagues). Plympton and Ken became great friends. Plympton had played a few games with the parent club in Boston for manager Joe Morgan and could do an excellent and humorous imitation of him.

The atmosphere in Pawtucket was a very positive one. Teammates got along and encouraged one another; there was no jealousy. With guys like Plympton around there was always a good laugh in the clubhouse and on the field. As he thought back on his career Ken remembered other players who were fun to be with and those who were difficult to be around. One of the most difficult for Kenny to be around was an individual who claimed he came from one of the local colleges in the Providence area. They first met in Elmira during Ken's first year in pro ball. Ken, the seventeen-year-old kid, was standing gazing in wonderment in front of a locker room mirror admiring his first professional uniform. He noticed this player standing behind him laughing. He soon had the whole locker room laughing at Ken's expense. Ken said, "I never felt so embarrassed as I did at that moment. I just wish at the time I was on some other continent."

Ken told me there are all sorts of ballplayers and they all have their opinions. Some just love the limelight. Some will attempt anything to get a laugh at the expense of others. This ballplayer in his mind had it all figured out. His "greatness" would soon have him playing third base in Boston. At that time though there was another third baseman playing at that position. His name was Wade Boggs, and he wasn't going anywhere soon. Boggs is now in Cooperstown. Baseball has a funny way of deciding the future of players and teams, like the

Red Sox selling *The Babe* or trading fan favorite all-star shortstop Nomar Garciaparra.

A few years after his Elmira stint Ken was riding as the front passenger in a teammate's car pulling into the ballpark for another spring training session when they spotted this player with a mean tongue. The driver shouted at him, "What's up, where are you going?"

He walked up to the car and stuck his head in the window and kept repeating, "Bagwell can't carry my jock, Bagwell can't carry my jock!" He then told them that he had been released just five minutes earlier, and the organization signed a kid named Jeff Bagwell to replace him. He kept repeating, "Bagwell can't carry my jock!" His mantra in sports terminology means *this guy isn't anywhere as good as I am*. During his tirade Ken sat with a smile on his face. He asked, "What's so funny Ryan?"

Ken replied, "This Bagwell is one heck of a hitter, I do know that." The ballplayer said that he would try to latch on with another organization. Baseball has a funny way … This third baseman quietly slipped from the rosters of professional ball…Ryan went on to be Fireman of the Year….Bagwell became a true major league slugger. Baseball is funny like that!

Baseball is full of characters. During spring training in Fort Meyers, Ken was in the clubhouse with some other players when former President George Bush (Sr.) stopped in to meet the Boston team. He shook hands with Mo (Vaughn) and Scott (Cooper) and a few other players and then left. Ken said to one of the players standing next to him, "Wow! Can you believe that?" Most agreed that they would never have that opportunity again. Another player looked confused and said, "Yeah, guys, who was that man anyway; didn't he have something to do with the war (Desert Storm)?" His teammates stood dumbfounded.

TOSSING HEAT

How could anyone not know who the former President of the United States was? It just goes to show you that you don't have to be a Rhodes Scholar to play major league sports.

While Kenny was in Pawtucket he met Dick Pole, the PawSox pitching coach. Pole pitched for the Red Sox, coached for the PawSox, and later become the pitching coach for the San Francisco Giants. Pole would spend hours with Ken helping him fine-tune his pitches and get a better grasp on "pitching" a game as opposed to just "throwing" a game. Ken gives Pole credit "for making me a better pitcher." In October, the Red Sox asked Kenny to attend their fall ball program in Arizona. Ken wasn't too keen on the idea of spending more time away from his family and declined. Player Development Director Ed Kenny went to Pole to intercede with Kenny to change his mind. Pole told Kenny that only the top prospects in the eyes of Boston Red Sox are invited to play fall ball. Pole insisted that Ken go. "This league is made up of players who should make the big leagues. You can go to Arizona and continue to work on your pitching," Pole continued. At Pole's urging and insistence, Kenny played in the Arizona league. He blew most hitters away and ended the fall season with an ERA in the low 1's. His performance there really opened the eyes of the Red Sox brass.

Living on a minor league salary was tenuous at best. Many times ballplayers did not eat well. To save a few bucks they would skip meals and sometimes didn't have enough for meals. Most times everyone shared. It was part of the team camaraderie to help one another in tough times, on and off the field. Those first-round draft-pick ballplayers who initially sign for huge bonuses (as much as a million dollars) live well. Big-bonus players are the exception, not the rule. Most players were signed with a modest $10,000-$30,000 bonus. The average yearly salary of a minor league player is not a lot of money to live on, especially if you are or get married and have children. If a ballplayer is wise, he uses the bonus money judiciously to supplement his regular salary. Ken said, "If you signed for a small bonus, you made daily adjustments in your style of living." He added, "To 'make it' financially in the minor leagues on the salary and a small signing bonus, you made friends, planned ahead, and pooled your money with other ballplayers. We made sure no one went hungry."

One player who signed for a substantial bonus ($70,000+) immediately went out and bought a new BMW. This guy wasn't one of those struggling; he didn't contribute to the pool or help other players in need. All good things must come to an end and eventually his bonus money ran out and his high-off-the-hog lifestyle came to a halt. He began to ask his teammates for loans and to buy him a meal or a beer. In spite of his prior lack of contributions to the players' money pool, he was liked by his teammates and was allowed into the fold. Baseball is no different from any other aspect of human life…baseball had cliques too. Ken never had real financial problems in the minors. He lived within his means.

When Ken was with Pawtucket, the owner, Ben Mondor, knew many of his players were strapped for money. He would generously tell them that when they were on the road to go out and have a good steak dinner and charge it to their room and he would pick up the tab. It was his way of helping his players. Kenny said, "Other organizations don't do that for their players. Mondor was the exception." The players thought the world of Mondor. Many times when a player's career was over they would return to Pawtucket to visit him (Mondor) to thank him for his generosity.

Ken played on teams that featured Mo Vaughn, Phil Plantier, Eric Wedge, Scott Cooper, and Paul Quantrill, all of whom made it to the major leagues. Vaughn, at one time, was one of the most feared hitters in baseball. Quantrill became a quality starter and then reliever. Wedge eventually became a major league manager. Ken said he had many great laughs and has many fond memories of his playing days in Pawtucket. Baseball, like all aspects of life, offers a great mix of difficult and good times. Somehow the good times linger longer than the difficult ones.

Ken, like his friend Curt Schilling, was a fan's player. Both were always honored to sign autographs and did so often. He wondered why some of the high-profile players ignored the fans and refused to sign anything. It was the fans that helped make them truly marketable personages. If fans didn't buy tickets and root for their favorite players how big could their salaries and egos be?

August 30, 1992, was one of those great hot summer evenings, ones meant for playing and watching baseball. The PawSox were at home. Kenny was in the bullpen as usual. He was the team's closer. He was usually called to pitch when the score was tied or the team was ahead. His job was to hold the tie long enough for his team to break the tie or to hold lead and secure the win. About the fifth inning, an announcement was made to the crowd that Jeff Reardon, the Boston Red Sox closer, had been traded to the Atlanta Braves for two minor leaguers (Nate Minchy and Sean Ross). The stadium was silent for a moment or two then broke out in applause. The people in the stands were looking over at the PawSox bullpen…looking for Kenny. Some left their seats to see if he was warming up to come into he game. The PawSox were ahead by a run and many were expecting to see Kenny, the hometown kid, pitch here for the last time. One of the other pitchers turned to Ken and said, "You're going to get the call" (up to the big leagues). Kenny said, "I doubt it, they have other pitchers up there to close out games." Ken was called to pitch in the ninth inning with two outs and the PawSox ahead by a run. Ken picked up another save when the batter flied out to center field.

After the usual congratulations and backslapping the manager, Rico Petrocelli, came to Ken and said, "Listen, Ken, I have to speak to you right now, I have good news for you." Petrocelli walked Ken off the backside of the mound and broke the news to him. "Ken, you got the call to the major leagues, you've made it to *the show.* Boston wants you to join the team as soon as possible. You're leaving on a flight for Seattle as soon as you can get your bags packed." The Red Sox were on a West Coast road trip and Ken would catch up to the team in Seattle. Upon hearing the good news, Ken was mobbed by his teammates and they congratulated him on his move to the majors. This would be the second year in a row that he would jump three classifications from double A to triple A and now the majors.

On the flight to Seattle, Ken wondered how Sox manager Butch Hobson would use him. Would he be middle relief or a closer? He hunkered down in his seat and said to himself, *Why even think about it now…just relax and enjoy the moment.* He tried to sleep but the excitement and anticipation would not allow it. He thought back to his first game in Pawtucket when Hobson was the manager and put him in during the first game with the team. Would Hobson repeat his actions, would he put Kenny in tonight's game? Ken doubted it. Hobson knows the drain a six-hour flight made on a ballplayer. Ken was awake for the entire flight.

Ken reached Seattle on time. As he entered the Red Sox clubhouse the first to greet him was third baseman Wade Boggs. "Hi, Ken Ryan, welcome to the big leagues, glad you made it," he said. Jack Clark came over and said, "Welcome to the show, Kenny." Paul Quanrtill, who had been Ken's teammate in Pawtucket, had been called up just a few weeks earlier and greeted Ken with, "Hi. You've made it, Ryan; this is the last stop in baseball."

After the welcomes Ken reported to manager Butch Hobson. Hobson wasn't in the best frame of mind. The team wasn't winning and Hobson wasn't used to losing. He told Kenny, "Just be ready to pitch when I call on you." Hobson continued, "You're here to do a job, just like everyone else. Pitch the way you did in Pawtucket. You're a heat man (fastball pitcher). Use your fastball often, that is your best pitch. You have to throw strikes. Bases on balls will get you in trouble, that's how you lose games."

There is something to say about Butch Hobson and the players he managed in the minor leagues. When he was selected to manage the Boston Red Sox, Butch brought most of his players from New Britain and Pawtucket with him. Players like Paul Quantrill, Mo Vaughn, Eric Wedge and John Valentin were some of the players that Butch brought to the Red Sox. He brought players he recognized as "gamers," guys who could play ball, guys who loved the game. With these guys he won more games than he lost and was being recognized in Major League Baseball as a successful manager. These players wanted to play for him and were loyal to him.

The game that evening was not one Hobson likes; his pitchers were getting pounded by Seattle hitters. Frank Viola, a lefty, lasted an inning and two-thirds, Paul Quantrill an inning and Joe Hesketh gave up more runs in the couple of innings he pitched.

Ken and another pitcher had been warming up since the sixth inning. He didn't think he would get into the game but continued warming up in earnest. When the bullpen phone rang pitching coach Gary Allenson answered it. Allenson turned to Kenny and said, "Ryan, you've got the seventh (inning)." Surprised, Ken nodded in the affirmative and returned to his warm-up pitches. As the Sox took the field in the seventh inning Ken felt he was ready to make his major league debut.

Sitting in our living room back in Seekonk, Massachusetts, his mother and I were glued to the TV, just in case Ken was called to pitch. We were astounded at the start of the seventh inning when Jerry Remy (from Somerset, Massachusetts, a neighboring town and a former Red Sox second baseman), the play-by-play announcer for NESN (New England Sports Network), announced Ken. We couldn't believe that Ken would be making his league debut just a few hours after his joining the team. Hobson hadn't wasted time getting Ken some experience in pitching to big league hitters.

John Marzano was catching that night. As Ken threw his eight warm-up pitches at the beginning of the inning he couldn't help but noticing that everyone in the stadium seemed to be looking down at *him*. Most didn't know that he was about to throw his first pitch in the major leagues. All of those strange faces were smiling at him as if they knew something he didn't.

The first batter grounded out to the shortstop. The second batter flew out to left field. The third batter Ken faced was one of the best hitters in the league, a batting champion and a future Hall of Fame candidate, Edgar Martinez. If Ken could retire Martinez he would have had a perfect start to his big league career. Ken's first pitch was a high inside 95 mph fastball that Martinez crushed for a home run. Ken said to himself, *I just threw this guy my best pitch and he rocketed it out of the ballpark.* The placement and speed of the pitch made it a pitch that shouldn't have been touched, never mind hit for a home run. After that Ken gave up another hit and walked the next two batters; Hobson gave him the hook (took him out of the game). When Hobson reached the mound he said, "Give me the ball, you're through for the night." As Ken sat in the dugout, he said to himself, *What a way to start a big league career!*

The pitcher who relieved Ken gave up three hits and all of Ken's runners scored. In all Ken gave up four earned runs in his debut for the Boston Red Sox. It was certainly disappointing for him.

Back home my wife and I were devastated at what happened and felt sorry for Ken. The game of baseball is fickle and you never knew what would happen on the field of play. No doubt, to this day Kenny vividly remembers his disastrous first night on a major league pitcher's mound. But this is baseball; you have to accept defeat as well as success. There would be more games Ken would want to forget about too. Sure, the players will tell him to forget about it, that one game means nothing. This was his first outing in the major leagues; if he struck out the side, with no runs scored, he would remember that as well as being shelled.

Fortunately, Hobson put him back on the mound several nights later. Hobson wanted Ken to quickly gain experience pitching to major league hitters. On September 12, 1992, with two outs in the top of the ninth inning, the Sox were holding on to a 7-6 lead against the Detroit Tigers. Hobson called on Kenny to face the Tigers' good-hitting, right-handed centerfielder, Dan Gladden. This would be Ken's first opportunity to earn a major league save and do it at Fenway Park. The 33,000 Fenway Faithful wanted to go home with a win. They had watched the Sox come from behind to take slim lead; all that was needed was one more out…they were hungry for a victory.

Ken said he remembers the fans chanting and calling for him to get Gladden out. The fans knew too that Gladden was a dangerous hitter. He was known also as a first-pitch hitter. He already had two hits in the game. Hobson flashed the catcher Tony Pena a sign for the pitch he wanted Ken to throw. Pena dropped one finger to the inside part of his thigh indicating an inside fastball.

Ken set himself and delivered a fastball that caught the inside corner of the plate. Gladden swung at the pitch and popped the ball up to Luis Riveira, the shortstop, for the game-ending out. Ken had earned his first save in the majors.

On the drive home, Ken told me he was feeling good about himself and that he was glad that Hobson had enough confidence in him to pitch him in such a tight situation. Ken said, "Dad, I had to get that final out. I had to prove to people that I can pitch in the majors." Ever since Ken was called up to Fenway, I would pick him up at his apartment in Pawtucket and we would make the trip to games at Fenway together. It was during these drives that we would discuss his pitching. Nearing the end of the 1992 season, the Sox were not doing well but Ken's pitching was coming around. He had pitched scoreless innings in his last five appearances. His earned run average (ERA) was not too good but his hits-allowed percentage was excellent. The opposition still had a problem hitting him.

Ken's season ended on a very positive note when he was selected as the Red Sox minor league player of the year. This meant he was considered the best player in the entire Red Sox minor league system. This was quite an honor for a kid out of Pawtucket. In spite of this award, Ken's mind was firmly set on the start of the 1993 season.

Ken and his wife Odalys were thrilled with the extra cash Ken earned during his one-month stint at the major league level. He also earned countable playing time in the major leagues according to Major League Baseball Union policy. The baseball union is one of the strongest in the country. The union enjoyed a winning percentage against team owners. By union contract and agreements with baseball executives and ballplayers, a major league player's retirement benefits begin upon entering their first game. So when Ken entered the game in Seattle his retirement package was initiated.

The entire Ryan family could not wait for the start of the 1993 spring training camp. This year Ken would go to camp with the parent team and not a minor league affiliate. At least I thought that would be the case. Then, to my surprise, even before spring training started, I read in the newspaper and heard on the local sports radio show that Lou Gorman, general manager of the Boston team, said that Ken would probably start the 1993 season in Pawtucket. This was not good news and might only be grapevine gossip. You can't always believe what you read in the papers or hear on the radio.

The news was certainly a letdown for Kenny. He truly believed, especially after five scoreless outings, that he would start the 1993 season as a member Boston Red Sox. It seemed as if February would never come and the thought of another spring training camp with a minor league team was becoming a heartache.

Training camp for the Sox was at their new and greatly improved facility in Ft. Meyers, Florida. The move from Winter Haven, Florida, which had been their training home since 1966, was a welcomed one. They left an outdated complex that was small and didn't adequately meet the needs of a major league ball club. Prior to Winter Haven the Sox had trained in Scottsdale, Arizona (1959-1965). Ken had spent all of his time on the minor league fields of the complex at Winter Haven and hoped that this year was going to be different.

Kenny arrived in Ft. Meyers at the designated time for pitchers and catchers to begin spring training. This time, instead of walking into a cramped clubhouse where minor leaguers were segregated from the established major leaguers, where the minor leaguers had open wire lockers and a taped name plate, Ken found a spacious, well-equipped, state-of-the-art clubhouse with a real locker with his nameplate on it. This seemed promising, he thought.

After putting his gear in the locker, he reported to manager Hobson, who was sitting in his office with pitching coach Rich Gale. Hobson immediately said, "Listen, Kenny, I have no idea if you're going to be on this team or if you are going back to Pawtucket. The way it appears right now is that you are headed back to the PawSox. This team is going to carry only eleven pitchers and there are people above me who want only seasoned veterans on it." Gale sat silent. Hobson continued, "Ryan, just go out there and pitch and see what happens."

Ken was very disappointed at the prospect of pitching back at McCoy Stadium for the PawSox. He knew he was well prepared for the coming season. His arm felt great; he had started throwing the second week of January to get his arm loose and strong. He didn't neglect the rest of his body either. He had a regular running and weightlifting routine, his body was in good condition. He was physically ready.

After his meeting with the manager, he went back to his locker and sat contemplating uncertainty. Kenny knew that this camp would have to be his best ever. He did not intend to return to Pawtucket. He would show them (Sox brass) that *if* he was sent back to the minors there would be plenty of fans wondering why. *Let the show begin,* Kenny thought. *I can play with these guys.* Ken was issued uniform number 50, a number he hoped would be lucky for him

When the Sox traded veteran closer Jeff Reardon Ken believed that he had a real chance to become the team's closer...then the Jeff Russell rumors began. Management made statements about Ken's inexperience and believed that he couldn't handle the job of closer this year, brought a cloud of doubt about Ken's longevity with the parent club and all but dashed his hopes for the closer's role.

The signing of Russell was no surprise; the rumors came to be truths. Russell was an established closer and had been very successful in that role with the Texas Rangers. Newspapers now began to report that there was little chance for Kenny to be with the Boston team when the season started. Pawtucket was more than likely going to get its "kid" back.

Ken was understandably disappointed. He had worked hard in the off-season to report to camp in great physical and mental condition. He told me that he was going to make it very hard for the Red Sox brass to overlook him.

Ken's first nine outings were superb. He pitched nine innings, allowing three hits and one earned run while striking out eight. He constantly had a pitcher's count and issued few walks. He totally dominated the opposition. People began taking notice of the new kid in camp, the kid with a blazing fastball, the kid who was getting some of the best major leaguers out. He had the best ERA on the team, a sensational 1.86. Word around Ft. Meyers was that he had the best arm on the team with the exception of Roger Clemens. Ken had every reason to be optimistic.

Manager Hobson clearly wanted Ken on the team but management had other ideas. Russell had been signed to a huge contract and they didn't want to make him unhappy with some hotshot kid making the team. The new kid would not threaten Russell's position as the team's preeminent closer if he were stashed conveniently in Pawtucket. It was announced that Ken would start the season in Pawtucket and then *pitch* his way onto the parent club, probably by June or July. Lou Gorman, the general manager, was from the old school of baseball and had an excellent reputation as a smart fox and making good trades when he had to. Gorman had taken the Red Sox to the World Series in 1986 and some of the acquisitions he made that year almost brought them a championship.

I believed too that had Lou Gorman stayed on as general manager and had not been replaced by Dan Duquette, Ken wouldn't have been traded to Philadelphia.

Kenny knew the call to the manager's office would come soon. He expected to be playing at the minor league complex any day now. Another year in Pawtucket seemed inevitable. Ken got the dreaded call to meet with his manager. He sat in the chair across from Hobson and waited for the bad news. Hobson told Kenny that, as usual, a couple of days before the end of spring training the Sox leadership met to make the final team cuts needed to solidify the 1993 Boston Red Sox roster. Surprisingly, the Sox would carry twelve, not eleven pitchers. Hobson then delivered the bomb. Ken Ryan would be the twelfth pitcher who would head north with the major league team. At least for now, Hobson told him, he had made the show.

Ken knew that as hard as he had pitched for Hobson in spring training, Hobson had pitched for him with the Sox brass. Ken thanked his manager for his support and confidence. Ken also knew he had *earned* this spot by out-pitching many of the veteran pitchers. The Ryan family and all of Ken's friends both in and out of baseball knew it, too. A thrilled Ken Ryan returned to his locker to sit and contemplate. He knew his spring stats had won him a reprieve from Pawtucket. After all, how could you demote a pitcher with the best ERA in camp—a minuscule

1.39—a pitcher who had struck out ten in thirteen innings. To make a major league pitching roster you had to be very good...Ken knew he was good. He had, for the time being, beaten the odds. He knew that now more than ever before, he had to pitch well every time he was called to the mound. Playing in Pawtucket no longer had the allure it had just a few years earlier.

The interesting thing about that spring was that Jeff Russell and Ken were competing for the closer's role. Russell knew that Hobson had lobbied the Sox brass to keep Kenny as the closer and that didn't sit well with him. Ryan and Russell were in a death match for the closer's position.

The 1993 Boston Red Sox pitching staff consisted of some pretty impressive pitchers like Roger Clemens, Danny Darwin, Frank Viola, Jeff Russell. Paul Quantrill, Greg Harris, John Dopson, Scott Bankhead, Tony Fossas, and the Pawtucket escapee, Ken Ryan, completed the staff. Pitcher Jose Melendez also made the team but was on the DL (disabled list). Bob Melvin and Tony Pena would handle the catching duties. Sox defense also listed some impressive players like Andre Dawson, Mo Vaughn, Ivan Calderon, John Valentin, Mike Greenwall and Tim Neahring. Scott Cooper, Scott Fletcher, Carlos Quintana, Jeff Richardson, Ernie Riles, Luis Rivera, Billy Hatcher, and Bob Zupcic finished the list of position players.

Ken had no problems making new friends and renewing friendships with those he had played with in the minors (Vaughn, Valentin and Cooper). One of the pitchers, Tony Fossas (relieved Ken the night Edgar Martinez took Ken deep in Seattle), and Ken became good friends. Ken and Scott Cooper were the youngest members on the team.

By the nineteenth of May, Ken had made the most relief appearances on the team and owned a superb 1.59 ERA. His pitching, this far, was probably the best of his young career. At one point, in fifteen of his appearances he didn't allow a single earned run. About the same time rumors began to circulate that Ken would be returning to Pawtucket because Jose Melendez would be coming off the DL and returning to the Boston pitching staff. Some people thought Melendez had a rubber arm and could pitch often. He did spend some time on the DL while with the Red Sox.

Ken felt safe wrapped in his sparkling ERA and team-leading number of appearances...baseball is a fickle game...Ken was optioned to Pawtucket. Every ballplayer has options in their contact. Options are in effect for three years. This means a club can send (option) a player back to the minors as often as they want during those option years. Ken was optioned to the PawSox twice in 1993. Optioning a player sometimes has nothing to do with their performance. Ken was optioned once (in 1993) when he was 4-0 and had a 2.45 ERA. The option happened simply because there was no room on the pitching staff to keep him. Ken had the stats but Joe Hesketh was being paid a million dollars a year or more...so Ken ended up in Pawtucket.

The press wanted to know the particulars on why Ken was returning to Pawtucket since at the time of the move he was arguably the best pitcher on the team. Ken, always the professional, refused to publicly complain. He said, "There was no sense complaining; they will recall me when they want to. It's a numbers game and a business decision...I have no control." No ball club wants to look foolish, but some of the Sox moves that year really had the press pushing for answers. The decision to send Kenny back to Pawtucket really got them digging at management for answers. The press felt the move might hurt Ken's promising career and openly pressured the Sox brass to return Kenny to the Sox.

TOSSING HEAT

Ken's stay in Pawtucket lasted for only a few weeks. Many ballplayers that are recalled to the parent club are a bit off stride. The player at the minor league level is different and a returning player usually needs a short period of time to readjust to major league style and caliber of play. Fortunately for Ken, he returned to Boston and immediately picked up where he left off. Ken's 1993 stats were excellent. In 50 innings he struck out 40 batters, was 7-2 with a very respectable 3.60 ERA.

Ballplayers, like the rest of us, make friends at work. They go out for dinner or a beer after a game and get together on off days for a round of golf or some other mutually enjoyable pastime. Ken met Matt Young during his first call up from Pawtucket in 1992. Ken and Matt quickly became friends. Young was down-to-earth and on one occasion his generosity touched Ken personally. While on a West Coast swing, during their first day off, Matt took Ken to a high-class shoe store and bought him a $200 pair of shoes. An unwritten rule in the big leagues is that a veteran player helps a rookie. Young's generosity was one of the ways he expressed friendship.

Matt was liked and respected by the other players. Young came out of Seattle, with a reputation as a hard-throwing left-handed pitcher. The Sox acquired him in 1991 and during his tenure he had some success, including a no-hitter in 1992. However, he had a serious flaw as a pitcher. During his attempts to keep runners from taking huge leads off first base, the baseball usually landed in the dugout or in right field. He could throw to second or third base but a toss to first was an adventure. There was nothing physically keeping him from making the throw, it was all a mental block. Matt Young wasn't the first player with a pitching problem in baseball, and will not be the last. Young had some splendid pitching performances while with the Boston Red Sox.

Butch Hobson, the hustling and hard-playing former Sox third baseman, managed the Boston Red Sox from 1992 through 1994. Hobson's "all out" style of play had made him a fan favorite in Boston. He managed like he played and was liked and respected by most of his players. Though he had some talent in Boston, the team was not very successful. As it always goes in sports, the manager is always to blame for a team's lack of success. Rumors circulated that Hobson was on his way out. Lou Gorman, the general manager, whose job it was to bring quality players to the manager, became an assistant to some high-level executive. John Harrington, the Sox president, hired Dan Duquette to replace Gorman as general manager. Duquette came from the Montreal Expos and was expected to "work wonders" for the Boston Red Sox. A year later Duquette fired Hobson. Hobson's firing was disappointing to Ken. Ken had a lot of respect for Hobson and was grateful for the opportunity he gave him at the big league level. Ken felt it was not Hobson's fault that the team played so poorly. He thought Hobson was a good manager and got the best out of his players. Duquette's plan was to strengthen the minor league teams and have a ready source of capable players to call to the parent team when they were ready or needed. He was going to do great things in Boston. Duquette did manage to get the Red Sox into the playoffs while he was there. When the new owners came into Boston, they fired Dan Duquette and put their own man into that position. The Red Sox have been contending ever since. In 2004, they became world champions. It has been remarkable what these new owners have accomplished with this team. The new owners do not appear to worry about what it will cost to sign fresh talent and keep the good players on the team.

The 1994 season turned out to be a short one. Players and owners were at odds and a strike began in August. Players refused to cross picket lines so baseball came to a halt. The strike frustrated both the fans, who wanted baseball, and players, who wanted to be on the field. Players were losing money and pension credit and owners were losing money; the fans were quickly losing interest in baseball.

The baseball owners met to discuss the plan to finish the regular season with replacement players from their minor league teams. The owners wanted to show the fans how greedy the players were and that they were ruining the game. Minor leaguers were told to report to the parent clubs and play ball or go home, thus ending their baseball careers. The replacement players would only be in the majors until the strike was resolved and then returned to the minor leagues. From a veteran player's viewpoint, the replacement player cared nothing about the team or other players, just himself. Owners called up anyone they thought could make a decent showing on the field.

Many players were worried about crossing the major league picket lines. They knew what could happen once the strike was over. Veteran players could retaliate. Ken was glad he wasn't put in that situation. "You don't want to be a replacement player, a picket-crossing scab. It will only give you a heartache in the long run," Ken said. "When it's all over and you really make it to the major leagues the veteran players will never let you forget that you were a replacement player. They will ignore you and resent being on the field with you. You can never join the players' union."

The veteran players were the most vocal Red Sox players regarding replacement players. They spoke as the group leader publicly calling replacement players scabs. Replacement players were hurting the players' union. They also said that they were taking jobs from players who deserved to be on major league teams. Most of the veteran players refused to speak to, help, or interact with them. Veterans wouldn't even take pre-game warm-ups with them. Their only friends were other replacement players.

During the 1995 spring training Kenny said that one morning, two replacement players asked if they could talk to him for "just a minute." They explained that they had no choice but to attend spring training or be released from the Red Sox. Their baseball future was at stake. One player broke down as he spoke and had to be consoled by the other player. Ken explained to the two players that most clubs were using minor league players to fill their rosters for the upcoming season. Ken said the best advice he could give them was that you have to make your own decision on this matter. "This is one of the toughest decisions of your entire life. Personally, I wouldn't cross the picket line and play, but that's just me. I think this strike will be over soon and things will get back to normal. Remember if you are capable of playing this game there will always be someone who will find a place for you on a major league roster. The strike will be forgotten by most people, especially the fans, but not the union or the players. Players have an excellent memory. They can be very insulting and will remember you as a scab." Ken told them that there could be huge problems if they crossed the line and played. The union would drop them for life. For years after the strike, the players who crossed the line were often insulted and treated poorly. Eventually some of them made it to the big leagues but they would be forever scarred.

When I asked Ken about the whole strike issue, he said that he felt fortunate that he wasn't put into that kind of situation.

Lasting from August 12, 1994, until spring training 1995, the strike actually hurt baseball. Fans showed their displeasure in what they perceived as disloyalty to their fans and greed by both owners and players by not attending games. Attendance figures were down for a while after the strike ended.

Strike or no strike, Kenny had another good year, although it didn't start out that way. A few days into spring training, Ken was struck on the right ankle by a shot off of the bat of hard-hitting Kirby Puckett. Ken was out of action for the rest of the spring. When the team went north, he was left in Sarasota to rehabilitate. He said, "It was so frustrating to be left behind, but there was nothing I could do. The Red Sox were in no hurry to have me return to Boston." He continued, "I could have been back a week earlier and I contacted the Red Sox front office telling them that I was ready to come north, to no avail."

When Kenny finally joined the team, he pitched very well. He closed thirteen games and had a 2.44 ERA. The strike-shortened year was a banner year for the "short" man from the bullpen. Kenny's pitching had earned him the Rolaid's Relief Man of the Year. The Boston Sports Writers' Dinner held annually at the Boston Sheraton Hotel was a special one for Ken with his family and friends in attendance. Ken and Roger Clemens were honored for their pitching accomplishments.

I went to all of Ken's home games, as many of his away games as possible, and would usually stay with Kenny in his hotel. I tried to attend all of the games at Yankee Stadium. I would take the train from Providence to Manhattan and then catch a taxi to Ken's hotel. I'll never forget a three-game weekend series in New York. Both Friday and Saturday were night games and then there was the traditional Sunday afternoon game. After the Saturday night game, Ken told me he had to be at the ballpark early the next morning, no later than 9:00.

We were up early on Sunday; without explanation, Ken told me to bring my camera. There was nothing unusual about this morning; I had accompanied Ken several times to the club house at Fenway Park and had the pleasure of meeting several of the players. When we reached Yankee Stadium, Ken went directly to the visitors' clubhouse. Before we reached the door, Ken told me to follow him past the security guard. As Ken approached the guard, he nodded toward me and the guard let me follow Ken into the clubhouse.

Here I was in the visitors' clubhouse in Yankee Stadium sitting at a table with Mo Vaughn, Scott Cooper, and others. All of them greeted me with a warm "Hello, Mr. Ryan." WOW! Most people can only dream of a time like this. The players' greeting, for the time being, put me at ease. Here I was, the father of a successful major leaguer. You would think I'd be more relaxed with his teammates but I was in awe of some of these guys. Imagine sitting with one of the most feared hitters in the game (Vaughn). As I looked around the room, I saw all of the players' jerseys hanging, ready for today's game. The only one that jumped out at me was number 50, Ken's jersey. As many times as I had seen that jersey, it always filled me with a sense of pride in my son.

Ken saw me looking around and said, "Go ahead, Dad, take as many pictures as you'd like."

So like some star-struck kid I started shooting everything and everyone in the room. I was absolutely thrilled. Ken came over carrying two gloves, a bat and a baseball and said, "Come with me, Dad." I followed him through the clubhouse tunnel and on to the playing field of *YANKEE STADIUM*! Ken Ryan, Sr., and Red Sox ace reliever, Ken Ryan, Jr., standing together in Yankee Stadium. We played catch for a while; most of the grounders he threw to me scooted through my legs. We chatted about the great baseball legends of the Yankees and the stadium and the incredible feats performed here, like DiMaggio's 56-

game hitting streak, or Maris's 61 home runs, the exploits of Mantle and Berra. We sat in the visitor's dugout, then I motioned to Ken to sit in the Yankee dugout. The dugouts weren't any different, I just wanted to sit on the bench that so many of baseball's greats had sat on. I was sitting there with my *pro ballplayer* son on that beautiful clear Sunday morning, a morning where the sky seemed to blend into the top of the stadium walls, the entire park was a magnificent blue color…a blue we would imagine heaven would be like.

Ken had another surprise for me. He tossed me the bat he had been carrying and said he would throw me a few pitches so that I could say that I had hit in Yankee Stadium. He lobbed his pitches, any Little Leaguer could have punched them into the outfield…me, I just caused a minor air turbulence as I swung mightily and missed, three times. Ken, grinning from ear to ear, called from the pitcher's mound, "Dad, you just struck out in Yankee Stadium!" I thought to myself, *Yes, I did, but what a great place to do it in.*

This was a real role reversal. How many times had I taken Ken out to the backyard or a ball field in Seekonk to toss the ball around or do some hitting? Now *he is* playing catch and pitching to me in *YANKEE STADIUM*!

I was in another world; how could it get any better as a father than this? Millions of fathers would have given anything to have these special moments with their sons. God was truly smiling on me that day. I took so many pictures that my camera was too hot to hold. I knew I might never get another opportunity like this. Ken and I walked into the outfield up to the monuments of the Yankee Hall of Famers. Here, monuments to Yankee greats such as Babe Ruth, Lou Gehrig, Mickey Mantle and others occupied hallowed Yankee ground. I told Kenny how much I appreciated this special day he gave me and told him I would always cherish it.

Kenny, age 8, receiving an autograph
from a Detroit Tiger player at Fenway Park.

Kenny batted over 300 in his senior year of high school.

KENNETH F. RYAN SR.

TOSSING HEAT

TOSSING HEAT

TOSSING HEAT

KENNETH F. RYAN SR.

TOSSING HEAT

TOSSING HEAT

KENNETH F. RYAN SR.

TOSSING HEAT

That afternoon Ken rung up another save. For some reason, Ken always pitched very well against the Yankees. The men in pinstripes couldn't get around on his fastball. It was strange; they had the same problem with him that I had…mighty swings and nothing but air.

During the next home stand, Kenny brought me to Fenway Park for a similar, up-close-and-personal tour of one of sports' most revered playing fields. As we walked the outfield, Ken pointed to a very special seat deep in the right-field bleachers. "There," said Ken, "is where Ted Williams hit his legendary 502-foot home run." He said that Johnny Pesky told him that no one will ever hit a ball that deep into right field again. The day of Williams' momentous blast was June 9, 1946. It was a rather windy day and Williams got the ball up into the wind. It seemed to be climbing as it landed in the bleachers. According to Pesky, Fenway was known as a windy ballpark until they built the .406 Club. Before the club was built, the wind would come right over the top of the Red Sox business offices from west to east blowing out to the outfield. Balls hit into that wind usually carried a long distance. Oddly, the .406 Club named for Ted's incredible 1941 batting average blocks the wind and keeps other left-handed sluggers from duplicating Williams' home run. The Red Sox commemorate the feat by painting the seat a red or orange color which is in stark contrast to the "Fenway green" all of the other seats in the stadium are painted.

Very few people can say they toured Fenway Park in its entirety but I can. Ken showed me every nook and cranny, including the innermost recesses of the Green Monster. Fenway's left-field scoreboard is one of the last hand-operated scoreboards in all of baseball. The scorer sits in a chair and looks through a twelve-inch to sixteen-inch slat in the wall and physically places the numbers to indicate the scoring. Until recently the scoring changes were passed on by a runner from the scorer's box above home plate. Now the scorer is connected to the Green Monster by telephone.

I was very interested in the enormous volume of graffiti that has been written on the inside walls of the Green Monster, some dating to the 1950s. One of the most interesting writings was that of Red Sox owner Tom Yawkey himself scribbled among the names of Williams, Pesky, Piersall and Kilroy.

In 1995 Kevin Kennedy replaced Hobson. Changes were in the air. Some players felt that their jobs were in jeopardy. Paul Quantrill, a good "rubber armed" pitcher (he could pitch two or three days in a row) was the first to go. He was traded to the Phillies for an outfielder, Wes Chamberlain. Everyone was surprised when the trade was made, especially when you consider the quality of the players exchanged. Ten years after the trade Chamberlain is out of baseball and Quantrill is still tossing quality innings for the Yankees. Kenny said, "Paul Quantrill will pitch for another ten years. He's just one of those 'quality' durable athletes that just keep getting better."

Not surprisingly, it didn't take Duquette long to get rid of all of the Red Sox, except shortstop John Valentin, who had played for Hobson.

The manager and pitching coach decided to change Kenny's pitching style. They wanted him to change his outlook on the pitching mound. Why I don't know. Even Kenny didn't know at the time. They wanted Ken to pitch more like John Wettland, who was with the New York Yankees. Wettland was a successful pitcher and at one time pitched for Kennedy. Ken had his own way of pitching and he wanted to keep it that way. He was successful doing it his way and wanted no change.

Ken did mention to them that he wanted no change, and that he was the team closer last year and was doing the job. His curve ball was fooling most of the batters and they were having a difficult time getting around on it. Wettland is known for his excellent curve and hard-biting fastball. Ken had his own good fastball and had faith in his own ability.

Kenny would call me from Ft. Myers and say he didn't like the way spring training was going, that the coaches were trying to change his style. He felt after eight years of pitching in pro ball "I couldn't change if I wanted to." He was getting disgusted with the entire matter and wanted them to just leave him alone. When the season started he got off to a good start and saved a few games. That fact didn't seem to have any effect on the coaches as they continued their style-changing campaign. They would mock his delivery to the plate and his pitching mechanics (motions). Ken's early success began to unravel, he blew a few save opportunities in Fenway and his pitching became progressively erratic. He knew he was pitching himself out of the closer's role. He told me that there were no excuses; he was not comfortable with the new manager, the coaches or their treatment of him. He said he just didn't feel right. He got so concerned about his pitching that he even tried their style, but that simply did not fit Kenny. His game-closing ratio was still good but by the end of the first month or so of the season Ken was taken out of the closer's role and was used sparingly from then on.

Kennedy and Duquette felt Kenny should be returned to the minors. They called Ken into the manager's office and Kennedy gave him the bad news. Kennedy said he would be going back to double A ball in New Britain (Connecticut) and work with pitching coach Al Nipper. Ken didn't think his pitching was bad enough to require a demotion to the minor leagues, never mind double A ball. *Why not the PawSox?* he thought.

Kennedy told him that his last few innings with Boston were sub-par and that he was walking too many batters. Ken was told that his stay in New Britain would be short and as soon as his pitching improved he'd be recalled to Boston. "I thought they'd stay with me a little longer than they did," Ken remarked.

After a few weeks Nipper was with another baseball organization and Ken was sent to the PawSox.

Ken was recalled to Boston in September. The Sox had captured the Eastern Division title and wanted another arm in the bullpen to take some of the pressure off other relievers. Ken was called into "mop up" lopsided wins or in a losing cause. He pitched well and didn't allow a run to cross the plate. He began feeling good about his pitching and himself. He stayed with the Sox through the end of the season and he was hoping to make the playoff roster. The Sox management hadn't said anything about it to him, so he went to Kennedy's office to ask if he was going to be with the team for the playoffs.

Kennedy flatly told Kenny that he was done for the season and that he wouldn't even make the outside waiting list. This was a list of standby players, not in uniform, in case a playoff roster player was injured.

Ken had faced many disappointments in his career but this one was a difficult one to swallow. After much thought, Ken realized he could only blame himself for his poor season.

Baseball is a business.

The Sox didn't get far in the 1995 playoffs so the dream of a World Series in Bean Town (Boston) would have to wait for yet another year. Rumors about Kenny's trade before the 1996 spring training camp were everywhere. Ken knew his days in Boston were numbered. The Red Sox management told the press that Ken had a major problem pitching in Fenway Park and the problem stemmed from Ken's inability to pitch in front of hometown fans. They pointed out that Ken's ERA on the road was excellent, somewhere in the low .2's, and that his ERA at home rocketed into the .5's. Ken just wasn't a fit for Fenway and the Red Sox. It was said that Ken might be headed to a National League team, most likely the Philadelphia Phillies. The Phillies played "old-fashioned" baseball, they liked to bunt, run and steal bases. This style was very different from the more conservative, big-score, designated-hitter style of the American League. Ken said he liked playing for the Red Sox during the last four years and had many fond memories but if he was traded he wanted to go to a National League team.

Near the end of January 1996 Ken was traded to the Phillies for relief pitcher Heathcliff Slocum. Ken was slated to be the set-up man for the Phillies closer, Ricky Bottalico. Bottalico, another blazing fastball pitcher, had been the Phillies "closer in waiting" just as Ken had been with the Sox in 1991.

Ken and I talked about the trade and he understood it as part of baseball business but was not happy about leaving the Red Sox organization. In '94 he won the Rolaids Fireman of the Year award and had the best ERA on the team. He had a good 1993 season. I could never understand why they quit on him so sudden. But then again I'm his father. Ten years is a long time to be with a baseball organization. How could they give up on him so quickly? I felt that after ten years in the Red Sox organization they could have evaluated him more closely.

Ken's stats while with the Red Sox weren't stats that most teams would trade away. He was nine and nine with 22 saves and a 3.66 ERA to go along with 137 innings pitched while giving up only 127 hits and notching 120 strikeouts. Most teams would love a hard thrower with fewer hits than innings pitched. The general manager wanted to be able to say that *he* built the team. Ken and I often talked about what would have happened if he was not traded and stayed with the Red Sox. Would he have had that special year in 1996? Perhaps the left-field wall in Fenway would have brought doom to Kenny as it did so many other pitchers. Duquette saved fan favorite Tim Wakefield from the scrap heap and brought Pedro Martinez to the Sox. Losing Roger Clemens to free agency was a real blow to the Red Sox fans. I'm not sure if Clemens was ever really happy here in Boston. I guess he thought he needed a change and leaving Boston might be the way to go. Well, he was correct; he pitched better with Toronto, New York and Houston, claiming four more Cy Young Awards to place in his trophy room. I never saw a better pitcher in my life than Roger Clemens. I spoke to Roger on several different occasions in the clubhouse and he was always polite and friendly.

Many thoughts went through Ken's mind as he pulled into the Phillies' training camp at Clearwater Stadium in Clearwater, Florida. His new manager would be Jim Fregosi, a former big league player with a no-nonsense reputation among his players. Fregosi was well liked by his team. They liked his hard-nosed style of play. As Ken entered the room, he was greeted warmly by some of his new teammates. Leading the pack was Curt Schilling and Danny Dalton. The "heart of the Phillies line-up," Lenny Dykstra, was close behind. "This warm greeting made me feel very comfortable," Ken said. He continued, "There are times when you report to a club as new player when things can be difficult." The Boston clubhouse house was a difficult place for a new guy...*unless you were a name player.* Most of the Red Sox players didn't make things easy on a new guy or a guy deemed to be below their caliber...even if you had a good game. This sounds strange, but it is true. But this occurs on many big league teams.

In the Phillies clubhouse Ken felt at home immediately. Ken liked being reunited with Schilling and they talked about their time in the minors and the good and bad times in major league ball. They never envisioned playing on the same team.

The players told Kenny that Fregosi was a player's manager and was easy to get along with. He liked to play hard and to see his players play the same way. Work hard, play hard, always do your best and he never bothered you. Like all managers he hated to lose, yet unlike some managers, he didn't always blame his players for a loss! The spring of 1996 was a disaster for Kenny. His pitching was terrible, yet to Ken's amazement, Fregosi stuck with him. Every time he pitched, he was hit hard and gave up runs. His fellow pitchers began to question the ability of the new guy from the Red Sox. Ken said, "Dad, I know some of the guys are saying this Ken Ryan can't get anybody out." This was his worst spring training and he knew he had to improve very quickly or face a demotion to the minors or a possible outright release.

On the surface his pitching seemed to be the same as it was in the past. Kenny said, "My mechanics are the same but I'm not throwing the ball with the overpowering velocity I once had. Once I get my speed back I'll be okay," he continued.

Fregosi was supportive and understanding. He said, "Don't worry about what is happening now, you'll come around soon." He told Kenny that most hard-throwing pitchers take longer to get ready for the season because they have to strengthen their arms. Fregosi wasn't concerned about the runs he gave up in spring training. He wanted Kenny to "just keep throwing fastballs."

The last game of spring training, the Phillies played the Baltimore Orioles in their new stadium, Camden Yards. Ken was called to pitch the seventh inning. At this point he knew he was on thin ice. Did he make the team or would a release be waiting for him after the game? After his dismal spring training a release wouldn't come as a surprise. Ken's mom and I had left Clearwater to make the trip to Philadelphia for the home opener scheduled for the next day. As we drove through North Carolina, I tried to get the Phillies/Baltimore game on the radio. We were able to find the station just in time to hear the announcer say, "Now pitching for the Phillies, Ken Ryan." We waited intently for Ken's first pitch and prayed for a good outing for him. We knew his tenuous situation on the pitching staff and hoped for the best. It was very annoying to have the radio signal grow weaker or be interrupted by static. At times, we heard nothing and other times we could barely hear the broadcast. At least we knew Ken was pitching. As we drove north, the reception grew steadily stronger. Unfortunately, the first thing we heard clearly in over 200 miles was that Ken was in a very serious jam. He faced a bases-loaded situation with no outs. I looked over at his mom and the look in our eyes read the same: "hope he can pitch himself out of this mess." Is it part of the human condition that when things begin to go bad they go bad in every imaginable and unimaginable way? Misfortune seems to last forever during these periods. The announcer didn't need to remind us of Ken's troubles as he told the listeners that "Ryan hasn't pitched well this spring. In his last outing he gave up three runs in just a third of an inning." As he finished that statement of doom and gloom to return to the play by play he said, "There's a shot out to centerfield, it's over the centerfielder's head and rolling to the wall. Three runs will score." Twenty minutes later Ken was sent to the showers after another disastrous pitching performance. Baltimore whacked him for a total of seven runs…all earned. As Ken handed the ball to the pitching coach and strode off the mound, the broadcaster, in a gross understatement, commented, "Ryan didn't seem to have his good fastball today. His ball had nothing on it. He had better get his act together or he could be sent back to the minors." *Can it get any worse than this?* Ken asked himself.

My wife and I had a hard time comprehending the whole situation. Every outing resembled the last miserable one. How much longer could Fregosi keep him on the roster? What was the matter with him? I knew he could improve…but when? He certainly wasn't getting the reliever/closer's job done. If he couldn't get through one inning how could he come in to shut the opposition down for two or possibly three? At this point, he couldn't get anybody out and really wondered if he would see any more innings from Fregosi. Ken said that after that miserable Baltimore performance he was met in the dugout by Fregosi, who said, "Nice job, Ryan. Get all of those hits out of your arm now; MY GOD, you can't have many left."

Ken rented an apartment in New Jersey close to Vets Stadium, home of the Philadelphia Phillies. When I first saw the stadium, I thought it looked like a building that had sunk into the ground. It sure didn't have the coziness of Fenway Park. Philly fans liked the park. The place grew on me during Ken's four-year stint. The seats were very comfortable which made watching the game more enjoyable.

When the season opened, Kenny sat the bench wondering why he hadn't been called on. He didn't take the mound until the seventh game. It was a cold spring night, the Phillies were ahead by a couple of runs when the bullpen phone rang and Ken was told that he would pitch the eighth inning. As he warmed up, he prayed that he would have a good outing. *Just go out there and pitch like you did in Boston, get the job done, get out of the inning without any damage,* he told himself.

At the start of the eighth inning, as he walked to the mound he was surprised to see that the ballpark was nearly empty. This was a new experience. Fenway was always packed. The many empty seats of Vets Stadium looked like thousands of opened mouths gasping for breath. Ken retired the side in order. He admitted later that "I threw the ball okay but my fastball was a little stale." He knew he had to be pretty sharp if he was going to do well against National League hitters. "I have a lot to prove this year and I just might make the Red Sox sorry they traded me," he said. Ken continued to pitch well and his arm grew stronger.

More importantly he was throwing with authority, he regained his fastball and his curveball was freezing batters. By the time the batter was able to determine if the ball was going to cross the plate it was too late to make contact that resulted in anything but a foul ball. By the middle of May he pitched fourteen innings, allowed only three hits and struck out fourteen. It soon got around the league that Ryan and his hard fastball were back. His fastball was clocked (radar) in the mid to high nineties, he was holding leads and setting up saves for Ricky Bottalico. Ken said, "I can't figure it out. I'm not throwing any different than I did in spring training when I was getting whacked around on a daily basis. Now no one can hit me," he mulled. All questions about Ken's ability to pitch in the major leagues soon faded. As June opened, his ERA was in the low 2's and he had pitched his way to being one of the most respected relief pitcher in the major leagues. Every time he took the mound he had complete control. He said, "When I leave the bullpen I am concentrating only on getting back to the dugout as soon as possible. I go right after the batters. They know what's coming but they can't hit me. It's like it was in Boston; my arm feels so strong."

The 1996 Phillies team was not an exciting team; Curt Schilling was injured and out of the rotation, Manager Fregosi was frustrated and the Phillies finished the year a miserable 29 games out of first place, winning 67 games and losing 95. Ken's pitching was one of the bright spots in the Phillies' horrible year. It was Ken's finest year in Major League Baseball. Ricky Bottalico saved 34 games that year; many of those saves were a result of Ken's set-up pitching. Bottalico pitched 67 and 2/3 innings, ending with a 3.19 ERA. Ken ended the season with 89 innings pitched, giving up only 71 hits and an excellent 2.43 ERA. Ken added to his value to the team by closing out eight games when Bottalico wasn't available.

Red Sox fans could only wonder what Ken would have done in Boston. They continued to wonder why the Red Sox Brass traded a quality reliever. Their answer of course would have been, Ryan wouldn't have had that kind of year in Boston. They'd repeat their mantra about his inability to pitch at Fenway in front of his family and friends.

Considering his '96 statistics, Ken didn't worry about playing in the major leagues in 1997. He would be a valuable asset for any pitching staff. We talked about where Ken stood with the Phillies and guessed that they were surprised at his great success and were very happy they traded for him. I told him, "Even if you never pitch in the major leagues again, you've made your mark. Most pitchers can only dream of the year you had."

In 1996, Ken was constantly around the plate and he wasn't getting himself in trouble by walking batters. One memory of that season really sticks in my mind. I think it was the last game of the season against the New York Mets. Ken came in to pitch the eighth inning and retired the side in order. As the last hitter flung his bat in disgust, we heard the play-by-play announcer say, "We have got to get Ryan out of there, he's killing us with his fastball. He's throwing in the high nineties and the Mets just can't catch up to it." It was wonderful to hear the opposing announcer pay my son such a strong compliment. It was Ken's last inning of the year. He closed it out in style and preserved his excellent ERA. Baseball was fun again.

I know that the machinations of baseball make a ballplayer's career a tenuous thing. Ballplayers are only as good as the last game they play. Right now there was nothing tenuous about Ken's last game or his foreseeable future…he had a great year. What a roller coaster ride Kenny had taken us on. Right now we were riding high and enjoying the thrills. The entire family would sip the memories of this year like a fine wine.

I have many reasons to admire my son but the one that brings me the most satisfaction is the incredibly professional way he handled himself while playing in the major leagues. When he was pitching poorly, he didn't look to blame anyone but himself. Many pitchers who experience a couple of bad outings or a batter who goes into a hitting slump look to blame the coaches. Not Ken. It was never reported that Ryan was blaming the manager or coaching staff. Ken took responsibility for his failures. He never embarrassed himself by looking for excuses. Ken always told it like it was. "I threw the ball, I'm in the game, and I'm responsible." Teammates knew that if they missed fielding the ball or made a bad throw, Ken wouldn't have a look of disgust on his face that you see on so many players today.

Ken's demeanor was always the same on and off the field. He was an intense yet an easygoing, approachable player. There were times when he got down on himself but there was always a smile and his pleasant personality. I never knew him to refuse to sign an autograph. One afternoon, just prior to the game, he came out of the dugout at Fenway Park and walked to a group of people down on the first base side of the field. They were waiting and hoping to get a few autographs. Ken continued to give autographs until he was called to the dugout by the coaches. As he turned to go to the dugout a young boy yelled, "C'mon, Ken Ryan, don't leave yet. Sign my ball, please." Ken went to the dugout *after* he signed the kid's ball.

Playing in Philly made it necessary for Ken to be away from his family more than he liked. When he played in Boston, home was only a forty-minute drive. Philly was six hours. Ken's wife and their children, Julia and Amanda, lived in our hometown of Seekonk, Massachusetts. To ease the problem of family separation, Ken bought a new Dodge van that seated eight. This would make travel easy and comfortable. On the weekends the Phillies were home, we usually spent them with Ken.

Odalys would pack up the kids and off we'd go. I'd drive and my wife Gloria was copilot and Odalys and the girls would relax in the back. We'd drop them off at Ken's apartment and the wife and I would stay at the nearest motel. On most weekends, we were able to get in three games (Friday, Saturday and Sunday) then head for home early on Monday morning. After each game, Ken brought us back to his apartment for a bite to eat and to discuss the game. My wife and I really enjoyed these intimate little family affairs.

Philly, like all great cities, has a nice selection of restaurants. Vets Stadium is located smack dab in the middle of the Philadelphia (South Philly) Italian community, so good restaurants were easy to locate. The wife and I soon found the best ones and visited them regularly.

I would often make the trip to Philly alone and would meet Ken after the game to go to one of our favorite eateries. Ken and I really liked the Philadium, which was only a short distance from the stadium and was one of the only sports taverns in the area of the other Philly sports complexes. After a game I'd wait for Ken to shower and change. The Philadium, on Packer

Avenue, was a place Ken and I frequented often. The food was great and it was a popular Phillies fan spot, so as soon as we walked in everyone greeted Ken with a "Nice job tonight, Ken" or "Atta way to go, big guy." It was nice to hear the fans congratulate and encourage my son so often.

Sometimes Ken and I would eat at the bar and "small talk" with everyone. It was a comfortable and friendly place to relax after the game. Kenny and I would digest the famed Philly cheese steak sandwiches as well as what occurred during the game.

This scenario wasn't new to me. During Ken's four-year stint with the Red Sox I discovered many very good restaurants. One of my favorites and one I frequented often was the Baseball Tavern on Boylston Street. It was across the street from Fenway Park. I'd slip in there before a game and being a regular I'd always get a warm greeting and requests for my son's picture or autograph. I'd always sidestep their requests by simply telling them that I didn't have anything like that with me. Like the Philadium, the Baseball Tavern was a diehard fan hangout. In both places I reveled in the friendly atmosphere and the love they had for their teams.

Kenny's move to the National League necessitated that he would hit in the number nine slot in the batting order when he came into a game. This was a new big league adventure for him. When he played with the Red Sox he never needed to come to the plate. In 1973, in a move to increase run production and bring more fans to the park, the American League instituted the designated hitter rule. This rule allowed the manager to replace the pitcher in the lineup with a player who did not play in the field. The DH (designated hitter) sat the bench until it was his turn to bat. A manager didn't need to place the notoriously poor-hitting pitchers in the hitting lineup nor did it force him to remove a pitcher who was scheduled to hit but was doing well on the mound in a close game. The DH rule allowed many big hitters, who had become less proficient in the field but could still crush the ball, to extend their careers and put more runs on the board, to the delight of the American League and its fans.

Baseball purists, then and now, feel that the designated hitter rule changed the whole face of managerial strategy. Until the DH, American League managers had to be true strategists. As the game unfolded the manager had to weigh every move with the care and precision of a general in a major military battle. Managers needed to anticipate the moves of the opposition for every possible game situation. The DH rule took some of this exciting and game-affecting action away from American League fans.

During one of those pleasant post-game meals at the Philadium, Ken mentioned his concern about his lack of hitting prowess. He had already made several plate appearances as a Phillie, all without success. He felt he looked terrible at the plate and realized opposing pitchers knew he was uncomfortable hitting. To them he was a sure out. He said, "Dad, during my time with Red Sox and all through the minor leagues I didn't make a single plate appearance. I haven't swung at a pitched ball since high school."

As he spoke, I reflected over his baseball career and realized that it had been a decade since Ken had had a bat in his hand. Ken was a very good hitter in high school but as a professional pitcher, especially in the American League, pitchers concentrate on pitching. No matter how good they hit in high school or college their ability atrophies as a human muscle does when it isn't constantly exercised. Ken was now being asked to use those atrophied abilities, and his lack of success at doing that was weighing on him. He questioned his ability to hit major league pitching. I could tell it really bothered him. Ken confided that he wouldn't be surprised if he went the whole season without a hit. He said, "Wouldn't it be embarrassing to go the whole season without a hit?"

Ken's first year with the Phillies was fun and successful as a pitcher but was a disaster at a hitter. Teammates knew his poor plate appearances bothered him and tried to ease the pressure by making a joke of his inability to hit. They told him that he may be the only major leaguer in history to never get a hit. Ken said to me that "If I could only get one hit, I could say I'm in the record books. I'd feel so much better, Dad," he continued. I really felt bad for Ken; it was always the same scenario, and he'd either strike out or hit a weak grounder to an infielder for an easy out. On July 1, 1996, his misery came to an end. Ken came to the plate with a determined look in his eyes and consequently lashed a line drive to right-center field…his first and only hit as a major leaguer. I knew, finally, that my son had gotten a monkey off of his back. I enjoyed seeing some of the players come out of the dugout to congratulate him. A couple of the players took the ball Ken hit and gave it to him inscribed with the following remarks. *First Major League hit: July 1, 1996, Ken Ryan, Eighth Inning, Veterans Stadium, Philadelphia, PA, pitcher Doug Henry.*

In the years after his playing days were over, Ken would jokingly tout his hitting ability. When the subject of hitting came up he'd grin and say, "C'mon, Dad, you knew the pitchers were afraid to pitch to me…I never got a good pitch to hit." Ken's "one hit" ball sits proudly, today, on a ball holder in my den.

People say that baseball is a kid's game. The following is proof that you can't always take the kid out of the major leaguer. During a road trip to play the Florida Marlins the area was threatened by an impending hurricane. Two games were postponed. The Phillies players reported to the Marlins' home field, Joe Robbie Stadium, to wait out the storm. Curt Schilling, who liked his teammates and in turn was liked by them, wanted to have some fun and break the boredom while waiting for the storm to clear the area. The usual clubhouse activity was to play cards or watch television.

Schilling had other ideas. He left the stadium and returned with a large box, full of paintball guns and ammunition. It must have cost him about a thousand dollars. His idea was to use the stadium as a battleground for teams of two players. Kenny joined Rico Brogan, Ricky Bottalico and others in grabbing their guns and ammo. The rules were simple. They play as a pair. Get shot by an opposing paintball and you were out. The entire park was considered the battlefield. They had the park to themselves and each team scurried off to find the best hiding or most defensible places. Ken said that there were so many places to hide it was impossible to guess where the next "enemy" would pop up. Schilling had orchestrated what could arguably be called one of the most enjoyable and unusual postponed-game activities in the history of baseball.

Ken really liked Curt. Schilling was a ballplayer's ballplayer. He was an intense competitor and a true student of the game. He noticed and studied everything that impacted it. He knew every hitter in the league and charted every pitch he threw. Ken said Schilling was one of those quality players who didn't think he deserved special attention or treatment. His easygoing and friendly demeanor made teammates and coaches feel comfortable around him. Yet Schilling was such a competitor and perfectionist that he wasn't afraid to get in a player's face for letting the team down with sloppy play or sub-par effort. Curt gave 150 percent every day. He expected other players to give at least 100 percent.

Schilling was very popular with the fans. He never refused to give an autograph or speak with the fans. I was at the Phillies spring training camp at Clearwater, Florida, in 1993. Standing near the playing field, I was watching the infielders take grounders when Curt spotted me and came over and greeted me warmly. He made mention of the times he and Kenny spent in the minor leagues together, signed the ball he had in his hand, handed it to me and moved off to finish his workout. He could have simply waved from a distance but he recognized me as Ken's dad and took the time to greet me. Ken at the time was playing in Boston.

Kenny said that Schilling and Roger Clemens are great pitchers because of their intense competitive spirit and their incredible physical and mental preparation. This preparation continues throughout the year. When some players see the end of the season on the horizon they begin to back off their preparation...not Schilling or Clemens. They prepare for each game as if it were the first game of the season. It's no mystery why Schilling and Clemens have endured so long at the top of the pitching charts.

Ken loved his major league career...all of it, that is, except the traveling. As a young single minor leaguer, travel was kind of exciting. Being a married man with children, major league travel lost its glamour. Ken hated it. He hated being away from his wife and kids. Hated not being there to help with family problems or participate in family functions. Telephone calls to home just didn't fill the void. While playing with Philly Ken constantly told me how much he missed home. When he played in Boston he was home an hour after a home game.

Just before the season ended, Kenny said, "Just imagine, Dad, if I have another year like the one I just had. I'm working harder than I did last year and will be in great shape for next season." He was talking as though he didn't want the season to end and that he was ready for the next season to start. But I knew he wanted to go home to his family. Almost 80-plus games on the road take a real toll on a player and his family. I told him to enjoy the success he had now and let the future take care of itself. Next season is five months away.

Ken wondered what the Phillies would offer him in 1997. He and I talked about it and I suggested that he try to work out a long-term contract. Kenny was successful with and liked playing for the Phillies. The organization, in turn, treated him with respect. He also liked playing for manager Jim Fregosi and said he was the best he ever played for. Ken respected Fregosi's baseball knowledge and the fact that he was a fun guy to play for. Ken said he expected Fregosi to win a World Series someday. Unfortunately, after Ken's first year with the Phillies, Fregosi left the team for a position as a scout with another team.

The new manager was Terry Francona. The same Terry Francona who, in 2004, managed the Boston Red Sox to their first World Series Championship in 86 years. Francona called Kenny at home in December of 1996, congratulating him on a great year and told Ken that he was pleased that Ken was on his team next year. That call didn't solve the issue of Ken's upcoming contract.

The contract details were to be worked out between Ken, his agent, George Bazos, and Lee Thomas, the Phillies general manager. Bazos, who worked for a New York City sports agency, had been Ken's agent since New Britain. Thomas was interested in signing Ken to a two-year contract worth almost two million dollars. That figure seems very small when compared to the money pitchers of lesser ability are signing for now. Kenny called me at the house after the contract was presented to him by Bazos. "What do you think, Dad?" he asked.

I told him to take the contract as it was the most money he had ever earned since putting on a baseball uniform. "This contract," I advised, "could perhaps set you for life." The fact of the matter was that Ken's record in 1996 put him on the "wish list" for most teams in baseball. He could have worked a contract with any of them. Few ballplayers ever reach that status.

Ken liked the Phillies team and the organization. The organization liked him so he decided to stay in Philadelphia, happily anticipating the 1997 spring training camp.

Ken reached another milestone as a pro ballplayer in 1996. After a game at Vets Stadium, he came to me and said, "Hey, Dad, you won't believe this but I just realized I've done something that most pitchers never come close to doing."

He smiled as a bewildered look crossed my face. "What?" I asked.

"When I pitched in Los Angeles last week, I became one of the pitchers that has pitched in every stadium in both the American and National League."

The 1996 success was partially a result of Ken's preparation, hard work, natural ability and new environment. Getting away from Fenway Park didn't hurt Ken.

Johnny Podres was the Phillies pitching coach in the '96 spring training, and Kenny credits him for his encouragement and his always being available when needed. Ken admired Podres because of his success in the majors and his professionalism. Podres had been around baseball most of his life, had a love for the game and a successful fifteen-year career. He won two games in the 1955 World Series, leading the Brooklyn Dodgers to victory over the cross-town rivals, the Yankees. He also once led the National League in ERA and shutouts. Ken said, "You'd be a fool not to listen to these old-school players. Their wealth of experience was invaluable to a rookie and veteran players alike. Some of these old guys wrote the book on how to play baseball," he continued.

Ken was fortunate, during his career, to have coaches around him like Podres and Johnny Pesky (Red Sox). They had so much baseball wisdom and could captivate a clubhouse during rain delays with stories about their playing days. Pesky had been a teammate and lifelong friend of the great Ted Williams and wasn't shy when it came to Williams' stories. Ted Williams had probably the most perfect swing of any baseball player in history. His ability to see pitches and command the strike zone is evident in his .344 lifetime batting average to go along with a slugging average of .634. Williams is the last .400 hitter in baseball (.406 batting average in 1941). Pesky said that Williams was a big-hearted guy, but don't mistake that as a weakness. His personality could change in an instant and he'd chew you up with a volley of expletives. Williams was a wonderful speaker and his booming voice made you pay attention. You knew immediately what his point was and that this was a man who knew what he was talking about. Oddly, for a guy who liked to voice his opinion, Williams had a real dislike for sports reporters yet in his retirement you could see him at spring training holding friendly and relaxed press conferences. Ted was a fixture at Sox training camps until his health prevented it.

I accompanied Ken to spring training during his eleven-year pro career. Each year I'd watch Ted stroll among the players offering hitting tips and critiques. To be critiqued by Ted Williams wasn't an insult and players were happy that "Teddy Ballgame" took an interest in them.

Kenny enjoyed chatting with Johnny Pesky, and hearing old baseball stories from him. I can only imagine what great fun it must have been for Ken to hear some of these escapades. Pesky was best friends with Ted Williams, Bobby Doerr, and Dom Dimaggio. They would dine, and attend functions together. It was a different era then. There was no free agency; players stayed with a team for years. Today players are gone after their contract is up. There is no camaraderie anymore, not like they had in the past. Today's players travel by air, some even take their own flights. When they rode the trains it was different and players were closer together. Players spent long hours on the rail dealing with their frustrations and wondering about their careers. Many ballplayers had second jobs to supplement their income. It's all about the money now, and that is why players leave their teams. In the 1940s and 1950s, team payroll was nothing compared to today. Players are paid so lucratively now they can be independent about playing this game. Somehow I have the feeling ballplayers of today just don't have the desire the past ballplayers had. So many players shun or report in hurt when the All-Star Game is played every year. I ask myself, *How can a ballplayer who is selected to play in such a magnificent game decide to ignore it?* What a waste.

I asked Ken about steroid use during his playing days. He told me that the "Don't tell" on other players was enacted while he was playing. Players didn't want to get involved in or have any controversy. Ken indicated that during the '90s there were players using steroids and other stuff. Because baseball has its own fraternity nothing about steroids came out until the recent book by Jose Canseco. Ken assured me that he had never used steroids or any other habit-forming substance in his life. He enjoyed a beer after a game but that was a simple relaxation activity.

I believe the older ballplayers of the past felt the real difference between modern and players of the past was their love of the game. The older guys had fun, a lot more fun. There was more self-imposed discipline then than now. The team manager was respected. Today's manager is lucky if half of the team is talking to him by the All-Star break.

Ken bought a new house in the neighboring town of Attleboro, Massachusetts, in 1993. The house was a modest home of six rooms but Ken added a room off the kitchen for a bit more living space. Now Odalys and his two daughters had a place of their own and a big yard to play and relax in. The girls were still very young and didn't attend school so a functional backyard was important. The house was only a few minutes away from Route 95; a convenient 50 minutes north was Boston and Fenway Park where Ken played for four years. About three years later Ken and Odalys felt they needed more room and moved to a custom-built home in Seekonk, Massachusetts.

Ken was now pitching for the Philadelphia Phillies and they, like Boston, took their baseball serious enough. Woe to the player who was slumping or not meeting fans' expectations. Their ire was not pleasant; they could be brutally hard on a player. Unfortunately, Ken would experience this unpleasantness in a couple of years.

Ken had had a very good 1996 season and was itching for the '97 spring training camp to start in Clearwater, Florida. Ken worked hard during the off-season to stay in condition, so everything looked bright and promising. He was ready. Pitchers and catchers are required to report to camp two weeks earlier than the other players. So for two weeks pitchers worked on soft-toss, long-toss, arm-strengthening drills and other leg- and arm-conditioning routines. Pitchers waited two weeks to pitch to live batters.

When the position players arrived, everything about training camp picked up. Pitchers could now face batters. Here the pitchers worked on pitching mechanics, pitch location, pitch speed and command of the mound. This was the time they tuned themselves up for the season. Kenny pitched a few batting practice sessions and everything was going as expected. He felt great, his arm was "live" (loose and durable) and he was getting hitters out.

Phillies manager Terry Francona told Ken that he looked sharp and to continue the good work because the team expected a repeat of his excellent performance in 1996. Ken felt little pressure and was eager for the season to start. He knew he was ready and confident. Nineteen ninety-seven could be better than 1996. He was a workhorse for the Phillies in '96 and he felt he pitched better when he was used frequently. "If I'm not used every third day, I sometimes lose something on my control," he said. "The more I pitch, the better I am," he continued.

Things were going well until late in spring training. Ken was pitching a game in Sarasota, Florida, and felt a snap in his elbow as he delivered a pitch. He said that the pain ran all the way down to his wrist and that he could actually feel the blood flow to the wrist. As he stepped off the mound he tried to lift his pitching arm to his waist but the pain was too intense. Kenny nodded at the dugout and then asked for manager Francona. Ken's first thought was that he had pulled a muscle, which was nothing too serious and with a bit of rest it would heal itself and he'd be back on the mound soon. He walked off the mound and headed to the clubhouse to be checked out by the team trainer.

The pain was getting worse and he was now becoming concerned. Sure, he had injuries in the past, but nothing like this. Several years back when he was playing for Lynchburg, in the minors, he had a bout of tendonitis. He was out for a couple of months but the arm responded well to treatment and he rejoined the team. This injury was different; he wondered if he had ruptured something in his elbow. The trainers said they didn't think it was anything serious, nothing a few days' rest couldn't fix.

The team doctor examined Ken the next day. Ken told him that he couldn't raise his arm above the waist. The doctor told him that he thought Ken might be developing some tendonitis in his elbow. "Rest it for a few days and we'll examine it periodically," Ken was told. Manager Francona, after talking to the doctor, trainers and Ken, told Ken that he obviously wouldn't be pitching for a while and to rest the arm.

Ken sat on the bench waiting for the arm to respond to the treatments and rest. Ken wasn't used to sitting around. The inactivity was starting to get to him. Not seeing any progress in the healing process, Ken had his arm X-rayed and later had a MRI taken. The Phillies' doctor, after reviewing the X-rays and tests, said he still couldn't find a major injury and insisted that Ken had a bad case of tendonitis. The doctor prescribed continued rest and treatments and forbade any throwing until he saw major improvement.

The 1997 season was a complete disaster for Kenny. After several months of inactivity Ken, in spite of the pain, began to throw the ball. He believed he had tendonitis and he could get through it. He suffered with every pitch he threw as pain came at the end of every delivery. He wanted to show the Phillies that he could still pitch and wanted to earn his pay. He was still being paid on a lucrative contract and he really felt he was hurting the team by not being available. He knew he was an important piece of the Phillies' hopes for a division title and a playoff berth. He also realized, though unstated, that the Phillies expected him to play with some pain as most players do at some point in their careers. Ken took the hill when they needed him until the pain was unbearable. He was concerned about his arm and the longevity of his career. The team doctor had no further advice. "Complete rest for the arm and wait for the pain to subside," he said.

During mid-season the Phillies placed Ken on the DL (disabled list) for 30 days and sent him home to rest his elbow. This really shook Ken up and he complained to management that he wanted to stay with the team and that sending him back to Massachusetts wouldn't aid the healing process. Kenny pitched in only 20 games for a total of 22 innings for the season.

Disappointed with his season and worried about the arm, Ken decided he needed a second opinion. Ken and I flew to Los Angels to meet with Dr. Lewis Yocum. After more MRI's and examinations, Yocum told Kenny that he needed an operation to fix the damage in his elbow. Ken would under go a "Tommy John" surgery for a torn ligament in the elbow. The now-famous surgical procedure was perfected by orthopedic surgeon Dr. Frank Jobe. After the surgery (1974) John went on to finish a 26-year pitching career. Only Hall of Famer Nolan Ryan has had a longer pitching career. Before this innovative elbow-repair surgery a ballplayer that tore a ligament in his arm was finished as a player.

Ken and I both understood the seriousness of the surgery and the impact the result might have on his career. Our next question concerned the rehabilitation process. Dr. Yocum explained the long duration and extensive nature of "Tommy John" rehab. Ken was told that he wouldn't be able to pick up a baseball for an unspecified number of months and that total rehab, if everything went well, could take a couple of years. I asked the doctor if Ken had a fair chance at rejuvenating his career again if all went well. Dr. Yocum responded, "Oh, of course there are no guarantees but this is no longer an experimental type of surgery and many ballplayers have returned to successful career after rehab, so yes, there is that possibility."

Ken was anxious to get the ball rolling and he was scheduled for surgery two days after our consultation with Dr. Yocum. Not wanting to sit around in the hotel room for two days, we rented a car and Ken took me on a delightful sightseeing tour of Los Angeles and the California coast. Ken had played many games on the West Coast but I was really surprised at how much he knew about how to get from one place to another. Driving in California is a test of concentration and nerves of steel, yet Ken navigated up and down streets, on and off expressways and in and out of several towns as though he was a native.

Our first stop was Hollywood. Ken narrated as we drove the magic streets of Tinsel Town. We went to the Hollywood Bowl, the site of many great concerts, and we saw the beautiful Beverly Hills Hotel. It was awe inspiring to drive past some of America's most elegant and famous homes as we drove through exclusive Beverly Hills.

Our next destination was south down the coast to Marina Del Ray, the beautiful seaside resort playground of some of the world's most famous and wealthy people. The marina was filled with the most palatial yachts from around the world. Ken and I had lunch at the marina and sat back and took in the breathtaking atmosphere. After our delicious lunch, we moved on to an entirely different style of California atmosphere, Venice Beach. It had made its fame in the 1930s as a place where weightlifters and acrobats came to work out. Venice Beach is like a 24-hour circus. People were in every imaginable manner of dress from skimpy bikinis to full pirate or clown costumes. It was Halloween every day at Venice Beach! Some people were rollerblading, others cycling, some flying kites and others talking to themselves. It seemed as though every activity that could take place out of doors was going on at the same time. I had never seen such a diverse mix of people or activity in my life. It sure was a far cry from the conservative beaches on Cape Cod. Ken and I realized that this was a fun place...but not our kind of fun place.

Our two-day jaunt along the beautiful California coast was over sooner than we would have liked, but the day of the operation was at hand.

Ken was admitted and prepped for the operation and I left for the waiting room. As I sat and waited for what seemed to be an eternity, I prayed for my son, I prayed they would find something less serious than a torn ligament. I prayed for his quick and complete recovery, one that would allow him to return to his major league career.

After the operation was over, I spoke with Dr. Yocum. He told me that Ken did in fact have a stretched, severely damaged ligament and wondered how Ken could have thrown the ball several feet never mind pitching a game. "It'll be two years before he makes a full recovery and can go back to throwing as he did before," Yocum continued.

After Ken came out of the recovery room and was fully awake the nurse explained to him that the reconstructive surgery was complete and he had a new elbow. I visited him later and found him not a happy camper. I knew he was depressed and really didn't feel like talking. I told him to stay strong and that he would be back on the mound sooner than he'd imagine.

Two days later we flew back home. For guys like Ken the healing and rehab are processes that frustrate and infuriate. With his arm in a cast, all he could do was wait for a start date.

In June of 1998, Ken threw his first baseball since the end of the 1996 season.

When Ken told me he would start throwing in February, I worried that he was pushing too soon and too hard to return to the Phillies. We talked about this issue and Ken said, "Dad, my contract ends this year and the Phillies aren't going to re-sign a player with a bad arm, especially a pitcher." He felt that with a good strengthening program, he could possibly return to the team in August and pitch well enough to get a new contract.

Only four months after surgery, Ken returned to his pre-spring training home, The Rhode Island Baseball Institute in Warwick, Rhode Island, to continue his rehab. The institute, at the invitation of owner Dave Stenhouse, a former major league pitcher, had been Ken's winter conditioning center all through his fourteen-year professional baseball career. Ken liked the institute and told me that when he retired he'd like to open a place like it. He said he enjoyed teaching the science and craft of baseball to all ages, so this would be an obvious post–major league career. Was Ken unconsciously foretelling the future? Did he, deep in the back of his mind, feel he might not make it back to the major leagues and was planning ahead? I'd never asked that question.

This spring would be different. Ken wouldn't be attending a major league camp. Instead, he'd be throwing a strengthening routine to a kid who worked at the institute. I asked him if he experienced pain when he pitched. He told me that there was no pain but that there was nothing (no speed) on the ball.

It was as if he were learning to pitch all over again. He knew it would take time for strength to return to his arm and the "pop" to return to his pitches. Ken had doubts about his ability after the surgery and worried that he might have pushed to come back too soon. I knew he had worked very hard at his home rehabilitation, but returning to the institute a mere four months after surgery left me worried. Dr. Yocum told him that he could begin soft-toss at this time and advised that Ken take it slow.

Ken did return to the Phillies late in the '98 season. He was ineffective in his 22 appearances. Manager Francona used him sparingly and never in a tight situation. His noble effort to rebound from the surgery and play a role in the Phillies' success met with failure. He just couldn't throw his signature fastball. At one point in his career he was throwing what ballplayers called peas, aspirins, BB's, smoke and heat (all euphemisms for a good fastball). His old, paralyzing fastball was a thing of the past and soon word got around the league that Ryan's fastball was very hittable.

Ken knew he wasn't getting the job done even though Francona tried to give him opportunities to prove he could still pitch. At last the season ended and Ken could only hope that the following year would treat him better. Many of our baseball conversations during the off-season centered on the question, "Could he ever pitch as he did when he was healthy?"

The '99 season was a bust for Ken. He pitched in only fifteen games and was not very effective on the mound. His arm didn't hurt but there was nothing on his ball. His curve didn't have that sharp break. His fastball had lost almost ten miles an hour and was constantly clocked in the mid-eighties. It was at this time that the Phillies sent Ken to their AAA team, Scranton Wilkes-Barre.

One of his teammates on the Scranton Wilkes-Barre team was a player named Steve Schrenk. Schrenk had been in the minors for over ten years constantly waiting for the "call" (to the big leagues). He had the distasteful reputation of being a career minor leaguer. Twelve years is a long time to hope in a sport that is age centered, especially for a pitcher. Some incredibly exceptional pitchers pitched into their 40s like Earle Wynne, Nolan Ryan, the Perry's and Roger Clemens. Most pitchers are in the twilight of their careers by age 35 and lucky to be around at 36. Schrenk was still taking the hill, still watching other pitchers getting the call, still waiting for the big break...twelve years!

Most organizations will give up on you in a few years if you can't rise above minor league play. Schrenk was having a good year with Scranton and Kenny said to him that he might be the pitcher the Philadelphia Phillies call up to replace a recently released pitcher. Schrenk replied, "Kenny, I will never be the one called up, just forget it, it will never happen." The next afternoon Scranton was playing in Pawtucket. Schrenk had brought his wife and family with him and they were visiting Rhode Island's "City by the Sea," Newport. Schrenk had no idea that he finally made it. He wasn't home to hear the call! Ken drove into the PawSox parking lot and learned that the Phillies had called up his friend Schrenk. The Scranton manager told the team not to tell Schrenk when he reached the ballpark. When he arrived, Schrenk was told that the manager wanted to see him. With a shocked but very happy look Schrenk emerged from the manager's office to the hugs and congratulations from his teammates. Schrenk was one of the good guys in baseball; he paid his dues, persevered through the course and never gave up.

Ken knew that this would be his last season with Philadelphia. At the end of the season the axe fell...the Phillies gave Ken his outright release. But a ray of hope was still there as the Kansas City Royals invited him to spring training. It was here that Ken knew he just didn't have it anymore. The Royals released him at the end of spring training, 2000.

Ken called me from the ballpark and said, "Dad, they released me. It's finally over. I'm coming home this afternoon."

Neither of us was very surprised at the situation but that didn't make it any easier on either of us. It was hard news for me to hear and I could only imagine how Kenny felt deep inside. Ken had given friends, family and teammates fifteen years of joy. Now he was through as a professional athlete. Later that day I picked him up at the airport in Warwick. He was smiling as we met; why I don't know, but it was probably to make me feel better. He said, "Dad, this is the first spring in fifteen years I'll be home and the first year I'm out of a job playing professional baseball."

In spite of his continued efforts, Ken's arm never came back the way he wanted it to. He didn't have pain when he pitched but there was nothing on the pitches. His curves weren't breaking and the fastball was mediocre at best. He just didn't have major league "stuff" anymore.

The upside to all of this was the fact that he was home with Odalys and his daughters and enjoying every minute of it. I was worried about his emotional well-being but he told me he felt fine both mentally and physically and that he was checking box scores every day.

No major league team showed interest in him but near the end of May ('99) he got a call. Odalys called Ken in from the backyard to take the call. To his surprise his old friend Butch Hobson was on the line. Butch told Ken that he was the new manager of the Nashua Pride, a New Hampshire team in the newly formed Independent League. Hobson said the league was a good one and was filled with many former major leaguers like slugger Pete Incaviglia and Casey Candaele. "Come on up and play for me. You're going to be my closer," Hobson said. He also said that this would be a chance for him to showcase himself for major league clubs. He said that he didn't think Ken would be in Nashua too long before a big league team picked him up.

Hobson didn't have to twist Ken's arm. Ken's baseball juices were flowing; he agreed to report to the team the very next day. Ken, after eight years in the luxury of the major leagues, would be back to long, uncomfortable bus trips and dingy clubhouses. He was back in baseball, nothing else mattered. Baseball can be such a strange occupation.

The clubhouse in Nashua was smaller then that in Elmira, Ken's first stop in pro ball. Hey, this wasn't the big league, so you couldn't expect luxury. Ken was just happy to be putting on a team uniform again.

As manager Hobson explained, the league was made up mostly of players who had been released by their major league clubs. All the players were in the same boat…they were all looking for another shot. These guys wanted one more chance to be seen by a major league scout. They drooled at the possibility a team would pick them up for another shot at the BIGS. The players knew that they had to play the game better now than they did in the past. An error or a '0-for' (no hits) could be costly not only for their team but their dream of the future. A bad night could send you home. A few players made it back to the major leagues. There was the slimmest ray of light in the twilight of their careers…they hung on, simply refusing to admit that they were finished as a major leaguer. This was a last stop; if you didn't make a team here your next stop was Wal-Mart or a car dealership. Kenny wasn't in the same situation as many of his league mates; he had been signed out of high school as a free agent and had signed some good contracts and prepared for his financial future. He had a cushion to fall back on. Many guys aren't so lucky.

Baseball was now fun for Ken. He played in the league out of pure love of the game. Sure he, like many others, would like to get to a big league team again, but this time was different. He told me, "The pressure is off. If I don't make it back to the majors again, so what, I had a heck of a ride."

Hobson told Kenny that he'd get his innings in and that he'd be expected to pitch the eight and ninth innings of close games. This suited Kenny just fine; he liked to be in the action of a tight game.

Butch Hobson, he still had that bulldog manner of managing, and the competitiveness that endeared him to his players. He managed like a field general issuing orders without smiling, and deeply involved in the ongoing battle.

Kenny was excited about taking the mound again and got right back into the groove closing games for the Nashua Pride. By the end of August, Ken led the league with closed games. The team was at the top of the league and was getting ready for the playoffs. The team won the title that year and Hobson couldn't be happier with his players or his managerial skills.

During the season, several major league scouts looked at Kenny but nothing happened. I spoke with several of them without letting them know I was Ken's dad. They thought he was improving but his fastball still hadn't returned to major league caliber. He was still being clocked (radar gun) in the high eighties and was working on his curve. He was also throwing a slider trying to make it a bigger part of his arsenal.

Near the end of August, the Yankees came calling and asked Ken if he'd be interested in becoming a Yankee. Apparently, the Yankees liked what they saw in Kenny's performances with the Pride. Hobson was not happy with the Yankees. He didn't want to lose one of his best players before the playoffs. Ken was the team's closer and the Pride would need him.

Hobson knew Ken was irreplaceable at this time, with the playoffs at hand. Wasn't this exactly what Hobson told him would happen when Ken agreed to join the Pride? How could he pass up a chance other guys were killing themselves for? He thanked Hobson, wished the team well and signed a contract with the Yankees AAA team in Columbus.

Though Hobson didn't like the situation, he told Ken to "Go up to Columbus and go right after the hitters, just like you did here, big guy." How could you not respect this man, Hobson? Kenny left for the Columbus Clippers the next day. Oddly, the Columbus Clippers were just starting a three-game road trip against the…PawSox! Kenny was returning home. He wondered what type of reception he would get on his return to McCoy Stadium as a member of the Clippers. The Clippers were hated by Sox fans as much as their pennant-winning parent club.

Kenny and I talked just before he had to report to the stadium. He said, "Dad, I always had success at McCoy, I'll be okay. It's going to really be fun pitching here again. It will just be my luck to get whacked around." Several friends called him and wished him luck. When we reached the stadium, Ken went directly to the offices of owner Ben Mondor and team president Mike Tamburro. Both were old friends and had played an important role in Ken's career from Little Leagues through the major leagues. They congratulated Ken on his return to McCoy and pro ball even though he was now playing for those rotten Yankees.

Returning to McCoy Stadium was an athletic full circle for Kenny. As far back as Little League, he'd attended PawSox games here. His call-up to the major leagues happened here. Now he was returning, trying to reignite a dying career. Would McCoy Stadium be the last stop of his baseball life? Was the circle completed?

Most of the Clippers players knew Kenny so he received the respect from them so richly deserved by a player who had a successful eight-year career in the major leagues. Many players fail to get beyond their third year. Frustration played on many of the faces of the Clippers players. They, too, were facing the realization that they were at the end of their dreams of a major league career. Some felt cheated that they didn't make the "bigs." It wasn't simply that minor leaguers wanted to make the parent club of the team they were playing for…they just want to make a major league team. The "parched" aren't too picky about the drink that quenches…any major league team would quench the thirst.

Most players in the minor leagues have never played at the major league level. When they start to falter during the season, they begin to try too hard, question their abilities and let frustration gain the upper hand in their performance. If they are lucky, a player with major league experience is either on the team for a rehab stint or trying to make a comeback themselves. These are the guys the neophytes turn to.

Kenny's success at the major league level made him the obvious "go-to guy" for pitching advice. Some of the Clippers pitchers sought Ken out to help them with a problem pitch or a glitch in their mechanics. His most important piece of advice was that a player's ability hinges on his mental state. Confidence in one's self translates into success on the playing field. How much Ken helped is a hard question to answer. The fact of the matter is that whatever he did, however he tried to help them, they had to translate that into physical and mental performance.

As the year drew to a close, these guys wanted to make a strong finish and an impression on big league teams…hoping that they might get picked up by one of them, or at least get invited to a spring training camp. Ken the tutor was, himself, trying to hang on, trying to fine-tune and impress. He wanted to get picked up or invited to spring training more than most on the team. He had known the glory and competition of the big leagues.

The International League was a good league. Teams featured good hitting just waiting to feast on inexperienced or over-the-hill pitchers. Ken knew he didn't fit the first category and truly hoped he didn't become a hitter's buffet. At least his first start back would be here at McCoy. To Ken pitching here was like pitching in his backyard. He loved McCoy Stadium. He was told to warm up during the seventh inning. "Now pitching for Columbus, Ken Ryan," brought a loud standing ovation from the packed stadium. One of their own had returned home, albeit in pin stripes. The ovation he got was awesome.

Ken pitched another week but things began to come unraveled. His ERA went through the roof. His arm simply died. The "stuff" he had at McCoy wasn't there, and his arm was sore. On top of all of this, the Yankees wanted him to finish the season at the double A club. They told Kenny they had a hot prospect that they wanted to see pitch at the triple A level. Ken being the last man called up to triple A would the first to be sent down to the double A club.

Ken called me and as usual the first words out of his mouth after "Hi Dad" was "Anything I should know about?" He always wanted to know what was going on at home before we actually got into a conversation about baseball. This call was the same except our baseball conversation had finality about it. He said, "Dad, I'm coming home. I'm through as a baseball player. No more traveling and being away from my family. From now on, I want to be with you guys when there is a BBQ or other family functions." He continued, "I told the Yankees management that I wouldn't go to a double A club and that I was retiring from the game. It's really over now...I'll be home later tonight."

I knew he was done. A firmness filled his tone of voice. I also noticed a joyous tone. He knew the end was here, accepted it, and took a measure of joy that it finally was evident. No more trying one last time, no more trying to prove to himself and others that he could still play the game. No more torment of a poor season, no more long road trips and separation from his family. His wife and kids were thrilled.

The local paper wrote a simple and respectful piece about his retirement from the game he so loved.

The game had provided him with a very good living. It took him to places only baseball could have taken him. He played with and knew well some of the game's greats. It was an incredible ride. It was over! Fifteen years of professional baseball.

Ken probably could have been assigned a coaching position in the minor leagues. Ken said, "If I'm going to coach in the minors, I might as well stay and pitch for some team. The traveling is one of the main reasons I left baseball."

His answer was always the same, "I'm retired." Kenny didn't want to coach or get back into baseball. The "ball" he now enjoyed was coaching his daughters' softball team in Seekonk.

There is a saying in baseball I heard many times: *Everyone loves a ballplayer.* Ballplayers are known for the stories they tell. Their stories can range from what occurred between the players and with the fans that come to see them play. Most of them are fun and amusing.

Here in the following pages are some of the stories about life inside the world of baseball.

All ballplayers pay clubhouse dues. This fee takes care of most things that have to be done to keep the clubhouse clean, well stocked with necessary items, clean uniforms and, of course, provide the post-game meal. After a hard day on the diamond, players come in to shower, change to street clothes, and enjoy a good meal. Since I had permission from the manager (Butch Hobson) I attended several of these post-game meals.

Post-game meals are a gastronomic delight. The cuisine for the meals is varied and depends on the city, regional fare, season, and expertise of the catering company. Only the top caterers from the best hotels and restaurants in each city are used. Post-game meals are interesting in that this is a time the guys would sit, relax and talk about the game or make small talk about families.

The table would be beautifully laid out with several main dish choices. Roast beef, lamb chops, steak, pasta, and specialty chicken dishes were favorites. Many times after a Friday game, fish and seafood dishes were added to the menu. In Boston, it was not unusual to see lobster on the table. The meal included numerous side dishes, a nice selection of fresh breads and three or four salad choices. To top it all off, an incredible assortment of gourmet pastries covered the dessert cart.

Some of the big names on the team were also big eaters. I can't ever recall Hobson stuffing himself. He was always in his office with his coaches going over the day's events and evaluating the team's performance. The team results were more important than eating at the moment. I asked Ken which team had the best post-game food, Boston or Philly. Kenny thought Boston had the best seafood and beef but Philly had the best Italian food. Since Kenny is half-Italian he loved ethnically rich South Philly. This strong Italian neighborhood was a short walk from Vets Stadium. Ken and I often walked to a favorite

Italian restaurant to wash down a delicious meatball sandwich with a cold beer after a game. It isn't a mystery why Ken never lost weight during his big league playing days. They certainly were fun days for Ken and me.

A majority of major league ballplayers are married with kids and are not really any different from the average American family. They have the same problems with kids' schoolwork, chores around the house and managing a career and relationship that keeps them from the family for extended periods of time. Off days are something players relish. These are days when they don't have a game or practice and can plan "family time." During the season, off days are few and far between. Players can be away for weeks at a time. A ten-game road trip is grueling on the body, mind and the family. There is little down time between games, lots of travel and hotel hopping. This steady grind of games, practice and travel wears on the players; they are almost always tired and often get bitchy. I've seen it in my own son, who is usually calm and good-natured. There isn't a lot of free time when you play 160+ games between April and September, more if you make the playoffs.

Add to that the off days that vanish due to make-up games because of weather cancellations and the season gets very long, very exhausting. Sometimes just having a day off can adjust a player's attitude and rejuvenate his tired mind and body. The only break during the season is during the All-Star Game break. This three- or four-day break is like heaven for players who aren't selected to the team. Some players selected make excuses not to play. Some say they are hurt, but really have no interest and just want to get home or take a short vacation. I always thought it was disgraceful how some of the players ignored the All-Star Game. Ken said that he would have been so proud and honored to be selected.

It is my opinion a lot of ballplayers lose interest in the game, and the reason is many believe the season is too long. The constant traveling gets to some, too. And of course when a player is struggling that doesn't help either.

When Kenny seriously injured his elbow he had time to reflect on all of this, and decided that for himself and his family, it was time to leave the game. Sure, the money is good and you play the game you love. But it takes its toll. There is nothing worse for a player than not doing well. Rehabbing from an injury or riding the bench due to a hitting or pitching slump gives the player time to reflect on his situation. He might think about calling it quits, but because of the huge salaries the players receive there has to be 162 games in a season.

I believe also when a team is going nowhere (not doing well) during the season some players relax and don't play up to their ability. Many players can't wait until the season comes to an end. Ballplayers are no different from other people who work at jobs. A lot of people just hate the jobs they have. I thought baseball became monotonous to some, playing this game that kids play for fun.

Ken played four years with baseball legend Roger Clemens. He truly respected Roger's pitching ability and competitiveness. He considered him to be the best pitcher ever. My son idolized Clemens. He wanted to be just like him and imitated his pitching style which featured a real hard fastball. When Ken was called up to Boston in 1992 his dream of pitching on the same staff as Roger Clemens came true. Clemens was the king of the team in Boston and everyone in the organization knew it. He was the Man; in fact, he was the franchise. The team was focused around him. Trades were made to aid his pitching style. Kenny said Roger's preparation for the game was astounding. No other player on the team prepared as intensely as Clemens did. Ken marveled at the man's physical and mental strength and toughness. Clemens never gave into a hitter or let up on his pitches. His curve could freeze the best hitters at the plate.

Ken's first spring training was in Winter Haven, Florida, in 1993. Ken told me that one morning before a game he saw that Roger was alone, at his locker. Ken thought this would be a good time to talk to him and maybe get a few pointers from him. Kenny told him how he admired his pitching and that he had followed his career and never missed one of his starts in Pawtucket. Clemens said, "Ryan, to be able to pitch in the big leagues you have to pitch inside to the batters, move them off the plate. Don't let them dig in and get comfortable against you. Don't be afraid of what happens when you do. Throwing a real fastball in this league means nothing to most hitters; they adjust to your style and take control of you on the mound. That is why so many pitchers don't last in the big leagues; they aren't in control of their pitching style."

Ken continued, "Later that afternoon, Clemens pitched several innings and I relieved him, pitching the eight and ninth innings. It was one of those days…everything went right for me. I struck out four of the six batters; I made great pitches and earned a save. I was congratulated by some of my teammates as I left the pitching mound. I really felt good about myself. As I entered the clubhouse Clemens was coming out, he stopped and said, 'Good game, Ryan. That is what I mean about pitching inside, you have to pitch inside okay.'" He didn't have to say anything to Kenny but he did and his choice of words stayed with Kenny throughout his career.

One of the most talked-about topics among ballplayers is hitting. Everyone likes to hit…even pitchers! Most major leaguers were pretty good hitters in high school and college.

For some that changes drastically when they make the big leagues and face quality pitching on a daily basis. Many of those great high school and college hitters become mediocre big league hitters.

Pitchers *love* to hit. The American League designated hitter rule has driven the pitcher as a batter to near extinction. Most purists think the designated hitter rule takes away from the game. Pitchers want to hit and most think they are really good hitters too. They still think they can hit the cover off the ball like they did in high school.

The purists say that replacing the pitcher as a hitter takes from the chess-like strategy of the game. What is there to really analyze? American League managers don't have to worry about a pitcher coming to the plate with bases loaded or in a tight game in the eighth or ninth innings. They are able to replace the pitcher in the batting order with a player who is a much better hitter yet does not have a field position during that game. The designated hitter only enters the game when it is his turn to hit. The designated hitter is penciled into the lineup where his bat will be the most effective. The pitcher never swings the bat during the game. The perfect example of the effectiveness of the designated hitter is the Red Sox's David Ortiz.

Many people liked the designated hitters rule because it extended the careers of a number of great ballplayers who could still hit a bit but could not play to the level that made them great. The extensive use of the specialist and relief pitchers did the same thing for pitchers, but didn't necessarily change the basic strategy of the game as did the designated hitters rule.

All minor leagues use the designated hitters so that managers have more opportunities to evaluate the position players at their positions and at the plate. Minor and American

League pitchers seldom, if ever, touch a bat. Pitchers just need to pitch.

Ken always talked about changing the designated hitter rule and returning to the original rules. He hated not hitting, and felt he missed out on a lot of baseball enjoyment. I always felt that the designated hitters rule was the worst thing that ever happened to baseball.

During the early days of his career, Ken and catcher John Flaherty were brought up to Boston at about the same time. Flaherty was a pretty good hitter and had a little "pop" (power) in his bat. Kenny and Flaherty had many discussions about hitting and Ken's insatiable desire to get his hands on a bat and show the team what he was capable of…even though he was a pitcher. Manager Butch Hobson wouldn't even think of such a ridiculous move. Kenny, like most American League pitchers, still thought he could hit big league pitching.

Kenny and Flaherty parted ways as both were traded to other teams when Dan Duquette became general manager of the Red Sox. Ken was traded to the Philadelphia Phillies, a National League team…Ken would finally get to swing a bat again! Flaherty went to the San Diego Padres.

The Phillies were at home (Vets Stadium) one evening playing the Padres. Flaherty was catching for San Diego. Flaherty was a complete catcher. He could call a good game, was very good defensively, had a strong arm and could hit. Ken and Flaherty exchanged pleasantries and Ken stepped into the batter's box. Pitchers knew Ken was an easy out and relished pitching to him. Flaherty said, "Ken, I've waited a long time for this. Let's see what a great hitter can do."

The first pitch was right down the middle for a strike. Kenny looked at Flaherty and said, "What happened?" Ken took the next pitch which was on the outside corner of the plate for strike two. Both Flaherty and the umpire were laughing at Ken's bewilderment. Ken swung mightily at the next pitch…unfortunately the ball was already in Flaherty's mitt as Ken ended his swing. Flaherty was still good-naturedly laughing as Ken returned to the dugout.

As a batter, Ken made the American League's designated hitters rule look like Einstein created it. He had his chance to "knock the covering off of the ball" in several plate appearances and didn't even come close to getting his bat on the ball!

Kenny first brought up the idea of a book when he was playing for the Winter Haven Red Sox in Florida. He called home one day disgusted with the way he was pitching. "Dad," he said, "I'm having a problem getting batters out. It's agonizing. It makes me feel like I don't belong here."

I replied, "You're going to have good and bad days."

"Hey, Dad, let's put that in my book!" Ken quickly shot back.

"What book?" I asked.

"The book about my difficult times playing pro ball."

I thought for a second, and said, "What about the good ones?" I told him he was just starting out and that his pitching would come around (improve) soon. After I hung up I thought it might be a good idea to keep the idea of a book in the back of my mind. I knew he was only joking about it, but I thought it was still something to think about.

Ken didn't broach the book subject again for a while. He was playing for the Red Sox and had just earned a save. As we left Fenway he said, "Dad, I feel great and I was really popping the ball tonight, wasn't I?" I agreed. Ken looked smilingly at me and said, "This one goes into the book, it's one of the *ups* of baseball." Whenever he was disappointed in his performance or when he felt he did exceptionally well on the mound he would he would jokingly say to me, "That goes into the book." The strange thing about the book was that after his career was over he never mentioned it again. Unbeknownst to Kenny I never let the book idea leave my head. I was an extremely proud dad of a professional athlete and believed that my son's story should be told. The more I thought about how he struggled for five years and how he had made himself a true major league pitcher, the more I wanted to write the book.

The PawSox people decided after 25 years of baseball at McCoy Stadium, they should give something back to their many fans. The fans would be able to vote and select who they feel were the best players that ever played at McCoy. Hundreds and hundreds of players were seen by thousands of fans. Some players were already retired and on their way to Cooperstown. Management wanted the fans to select only the best that ever played the game here at McCoy Stadium and who will always be remembered. Thirty players were picked. Wade Boggs, Roger Clemens Jim Rice, Oil Can Boyd, Ken Ryan, John Tudor. I am only mentioning a few. The fans remembered Ken and what he accomplished during his playing days at McCoy. I know Ken believes this is one of the best honors any ballplayer could receive, especially being in the company of such players.

"I have many great memories of my eight years in major league baseball. It had been a good ride. There were ups and downs but mostly ups. Meeting and playing with some of the game's stars was truly the dream come true for any American boy who grew up on baseball."

In 1994, Kenny was Fireman of the Year with the Boston Red Sox. In 1996 he was one of the best relief pitchers in baseball. He made 62 appearances for the Phillies that year, tossing 89 innings, and he led the pitching staff with a 2.43 ERA. He wasn't easy to hit.

KENNETH F. RYAN SR.

May 15, 1999, was probably the most memorable for him, and a very dramatic way for any pitcher to end a career. The Phillies were playing the New York Mets at Veterans Stadium. It was a nice cool Sunday afternoon, the score was tied and he was called in to pitch the sixth inning.

He walked the first batter he faced, Roger Cedeno, who then stole second base, putting the go-ahead run in scoring position. Edgardo Alfonzo punched a single to center, pushing Cedeno across the plate with the go-ahead run. He walked former batting champion John Olerud. With two on base and no one out he had to face one of baseball's best hitters, catcher Mike Piazza. He faced Mike a number of times before. He knew what to expect from him. He pitched him carefully and he ran the count full…three and two. His next pitch was a good pitch, a high, inside fastball. Most batters would miss that pitch. Piazza didn't. Mets manager Bobby Valentine had put on the hit and run. The runners were already heading for the next base when Phillies shortstop Alex Arias caught Piazza's line shot for the first out. Arias quickly relayed the ball to second baseman Kevin Jordan, who stepped on the base for the second out and then tagged out the sliding John Olerud, completing the inning-ending triple play. A pitcher couldn't ask for better defensive play than a play like that with the game in the balance. As he strode off the mound, little did he know that that triple-play pitch would be the last pitch he'd ever make in the major leagues.

As Kenny looks back on it now, he takes pride in the fact that he had thrown one of two triple-play pitches in Veteran's Stadium history and only the 28th in Phillies history. Since 1876 there have been only 660 triple plays at all levels of professional baseball. Only 607 have been at the major league level. Hall of Famer Brooks Robinson holds the record for hitting into the most triple plays (four). The most triple plays in a single year was 20 in 1890. In 1961 and 1974 no triple plays were completed.

Sadly, Ken's place in triple play lore was also the finale of his major league career.

Soon after Ken left baseball he started to receive calls at his home. The callers wanted to know if he was available for coaching or speaking engagements. He did attend several sports card shows in Rhode Island, Massachusetts and Connecticut as a celebrity guest but never thought about coaching kids on any level. Yet, he did have an interest in teaching kids the essential fundamentals of baseball...possibly opening his own baseball school. He always felt he wanted to give something back to the game that treated him well and he had loved all of his life...give something back to the great fans of Rhode Island and Massachusetts. I think this is something he always wanted to do. He wanted to interact with kids and bring them an understanding of how the game should be played. Give them solid basics in batting, fielding, pitching and the myriad of other skills need to be a complete ballplayer.

Ken became friends with another Seekonk native, Todd Treacy. Kenny told Todd of his desire to open a local baseball school. This was a logical avenue to follow because when Ken's playing career ended parents would ask him if he could help their young ballplayer with some aspect of the game. Working together Ken and Todd now run a very successful baseball school called KR Baseball Academy. The school's physical layout was well thought out. There is a very large field room where kids are instructed in every field aspect of the game and there are batting cages where Ken and Todd pitch to the students. The cages are also coin operated so that players not getting instruction in the field room can practice hitting at any time. The waiting room is comfortable with a nice refreshment stand and closed-circuit TV so that parents can watch the practice sessions.

When the Red Sox heard Ken had retired from pro ball they asked him to join their public relations department and be part of the Fenway alumni program. A couple of hours before each home game fans are able to get free autographs from present and past Red Sox players. It is a very popular program with the fans and Ken enjoys getting the chance to return to Fenway and meeting the fans.

During Kenny's years with Boston he met many ex-Red Sox players, and played in sporting events with these individuals. Such stars as Bill Lee, Rick Miller, John Tudor. And another good friend, Mike Welch, who played in Philadelphia with Kenny near the end of Ken's career. All of these players have attended Ken's KR Baseball Academy in Pawtucket. They came because they wanted to assist Ken, and get his baseball school off the ground. They all signed autographs and chatted with the people who attended Ken's open house. Bill Lee has not changed since he last pitched for the Red Sox. He is still himself and we all hope he never changes either. Just a fun guy to have around and very generous with his time helping friends.

Ken has told me on several occasions he has reflected back to that hot night in West Palm Beach, Florida, when he thought he was going to be released and asked the man upstairs for a little help. How this strange feeling came over him like he knew he was going to be okay, and that he was going to turn his career around. How he suddenly became a power pitcher, and rose from the lower minors to triple A. Three jumps in classification in one year. Mostly unheard of in the minors. And then accomplishing it again the following year. Ken told me not only was it a great ride playing major league baseball, but I realize now it is the ups and downs that made my dream so special.

TOSSING HEAT

Chet Nichols, a longtime friend and former major league pitcher, believed that throwing breaking balls as a developing pitcher was not good for a young arm (below high school level). Chet had a successful pro career with the Red Sox and Milwaukee Braves.

I took his advice and never allowed Kenny to throw anything but fastballs when he was young. He threw so hard, he didn't need a breaking ball to get opposing batters out.

Kids usually begin pitching in the farm or instructional leagues. Coaches look for the kid with the "natural" arm and make them pitchers. It is at this level where young kids begin to try to imitate their pro heroes. No one tells them that trying to break-off curve balls or other breaking pitches is dangerous to their arms. At this stage, their arm is still developing and the torque and pressure of throwing breaking pitches puts undue strain on a growing arm. Throwing fastballs strengthens the arm, breaking pitches does nothing but insure future injury to the arm. Sooner or later most breaking-ball pitchers suffer arm problems, some career ending.

Dads and coaches who want their kid to be the "ace" of the staff encourage, even push, the kid to throw breaking stuff. Imagine a kid not yet in high school needing Tommy John surgery! Yet it happens; coaches and parents are looking for that college scholarship or pro contract. With so many kids being signed right out of high school these days, the pressure is higher than it has ever been. NBC News recently aired a segment dealing with the issue of young ballplayers with arm troubles and the mounting numbers who need surgery.

The dangers of throwing breaking balls at too young an age have been known in the medical community for more than a decade. When Kenny was rehabbing from his Tommy John surgery he was being treated by noted arm specialist Dr. Bob

Shalvoy of Providence, Rhode Island. Dr. Shalvoy isn't a proponent of young pitchers throwing breaking balls. As recently as July, 2005 (*Providence Journal* 7/5/05), Dr. Shalvoy said that the number of kids suffering arm problems and ultimately needing surgery is due to the fact that their arms are not fully developed; they have poor pitching mechanics. The result is sore elbows and stretched ligaments, surgery resulting.

Since opening of KR Baseball Academy, many fathers ask Ken's advice on what pitches their son should be throwing. Ken's thought on the matter is that Little Leaguers should throw nothing but fastballs. Later while attending high school, kids can start working on breaking balls. Pitchers should develop a curveball during their high school years.

Ken's answer for the younger players is "The fastball. Have your son concentrate on getting the ball over the plate. The fastball is the easiest pitch to control and builds up the arm strength needed to make the adjustment from a Little League field to a regulation field. Kids have enough trouble throwing strikes; they don't need the added pressure of learning to throw pitches that are difficult to control. Kids who go on to play high school ball find that they are lacking the good fastball that would make them effective pitchers because coaches and dads make them learn breaking-ball pitches too early.

"You can't learn arm strength," Ken said, "you have to build it up over the years." He continued, "Pitchers can learn, with the proper instruction, to throw breaking balls and not have good arm strength, which is key to an effective and sustained pitching career."

I have come to the conclusion that the game is all about winning out there on the field. Doesn't matter if it is the big leagues or little leagues.

"Competition is intense, and pressure that is put on kids is enormous...not to *play* the game, but to be the superstar—the guy who gets the winning hit or throws the last strike for a victory. The games are videoed and photographed and then taken home for critique...adding more pressure on the kids and the family. Sports today are not the pleasant pastimes they were years ago, they are serious family matters. A kid who isn't the best hitter or pitcher on the team, the kid who isn't a starter, the kid who doesn't make the all-star team is an embarrassment to Dad."

Ken shook his head, a bit sadly. "Parents see their kid's future in college and major league sports. They know colleges are throwing athletic scholarships at good athletes, and they see the enormous contracts and signing bonuses professional athletes get and they are driven to make their kid a superstar."

Some parents see youth sports as just a stepping-stone to big money. More and more professional sports are signing athletes right out of high school and many parents think this is good, so they push their kids into sports and drive them to excel.

"The fact of the matter is that out of the millions of kids, both boys and girls, a very small percentage ever make the professional level. A good example of that is the kids and adults who participate in the martial arts. Fewer than two of 100 ever attain a black belt. Expectations placed on young athletes go beyond reasonable." Ken believes that in his area of Rhode Island and southeastern Massachusetts there are a number of talented young athletes. Some, be believes, could make it to the professional ranks. Ken's final piece of advice to parents is "Don't push your kids. Let them develop at their own pace. Forget the last game...it means nothing now."

When Kenny was sixteen he had a part-time job making muffins at one of the fast-food restaurants in Pawtucket. One of the other kids working there liked to joke with Kenny about how he was making the dough. Kenny told this individual that he had no intentions of being a baker. Kenny told him to look for him someday on opening day at Fenway Park. He would be on the mound pitching for the Red Sox. The boy later went home and told his mother and brother what Kenny said. Apparently they all had a good laugh over it. Just another kid with wishful thinking. Ten years later my daughter's friend tells this account. She was watching the opening-day Red Sox game one afternoon when they announced, "Now pitching for the Red Sox, Ken Ryan." She was shocked on hearing his name and seeing him walk out onto the field. She immediately called both her sons and told them to put on the Red Sox game. They were amazed as I was of what was taking place. She told her sons Kenny must have had all this planned out. He was committed to his plans and what the future held for him. My daughter told her friend that Kenny always said that someday he would pitch for the Red Sox. It was his dream to be out there pitching against major league players. The entire Ryan family stood behind him and backed his dream.

 I recently read an article about a championship Little League game between nine- and ten-year-old kids. It was the last inning, and the team out on the field was up by a run. The coach out on the field had a dilemma to deal with, and it wasn't going to be pretty. There were two outs, and a runner on third base. The batter standing in the batter's box was the best hitter on the team. The next scheduled hitter was the worst hitter on the team. He was a sickly boy, very thin too. He had cancer and had to wear a special helmet to protect his head. Surely if the kid now standing in the batter's box got to hit, the game might be over. The coach walked out to the pitcher's mound never speaking to his pitcher. He thought the situation over for a few moments and made his decision. He told his pitcher to walk the kid now batting. The next boy struck out and the game was over. The boy cried immediately after, and believed he let down his teammates. There were several arguments after the game because of what the winning coach had done. Really, was it the correct thing to do? The coach told everyone he did it for the players on his team. They wanted the championship too. Major league ballplayers steal bases on catchers who have weak arms. In the late innings they bring in their best pitchers to finish off a game. The bottom line is kids are taught winning is everything.

During the years with the Phillies Ken seemed in better control of himself. More at ease, the atmosphere was different. He arrived at the stadium the usual time, and enjoyed his time there. There were no issues that were noticeable between players. Ken never told me of problems with other players, so I assume there weren't any. Some people I talked with didn't like the Vets Stadium. Most of these people were from the Philadelphia area and they wanted a new park. I myself thought the ballpark was not that bad, and I looked it at this way, my son most times pitched well there. Today there is a new ballpark there, it stands tall and beautiful too. They tore down the old cookie-cut Vets Stadium a few years ago. I visited the new stadium the first year it open, and I was greatly surprised. There is not a bad seat in the house. Just wonderful viewing everywhere. They built it in the area of the old Vets park. So it is only minutes to downtown. There was talk about tearing down Fenway Park, and building a new ballpark for the Red Sox fans. It never materialized, and the new owners renovated the old park. I guess it is kind of difficult to tear down an institution that brought so much enjoyment to people. The Boston owners are still approximately 20,000 seats short of full capacity. I myself hope they never tear it down. My son can always say he pitched in this old ballpark for four years. And loved every minute of it.

Ken Ryan #51
Career Statistics – Pitching

Pitching Totals

YR	TM	G	GS	IP	H	ER
92	Bos	7	0	7.0	4	5
93	Bos	47	0	50.0	43	20
94	Bos	42	0	48.0	46	13
95	Bos	28	0	32.2	34	18
96	Phi	62	0	89.0	71	24
97	Phi	22	0	20.2	31	22
98	Phi	17	1	22.2	21	11
99	Phi	15	0	15.2	16	11
		G	GS	IP	H	ER
Totals		240	1	285.2	266	124

Pitching Totals Cont.

YR	TM	HR	SO	W	L	SV	ERA
92	Bos	2	5	0	0	1	6.43
93	Bos	2	49	7	2	1	3.60
94	Bos	1	32	2	3	13	2.44
95	Bos	4	34	0	4	7	4.96
96	Phi	4	70	3	5	8	2.43
97	Phi	5	10	1	0	0	9.58
98	Phi	1	16	0	0	0	4.37
99	Phi	2	9	1	2	0	6.32
		HR	SO	W	L	SV	ERA
Totals		21	225	14	16	30	3.91